# About the book

This is a book about a place that could be the most important country in the world. This is a book about how the Canadian circle can accommodate all those who choose to live within it. This is a book about how Canadians can help the world get along despite ethnic and religious differences while building an economy based on need rather than greed that enhances the environment rather than destroying it. This is a book about how Canada can be a model for the entire planet. This book is intended to be both a primer (soft I) and a primer (hard I). It is a short, easy to read (and fun?) explanation of Canada. But, it is also designed to be a small charge that sets off a bigger explosion of a new sort of Canadian nationalism.

A co-publication of
RED Publishing
2736 Cambridge Street
Vancouver, British Columbia V5K 1L7 and
Fernwood Publishing
32 Oceanvista Lane
Black Point, Nova Scotia B0J 1B0
and 748 Broadway Avenue, Winnipeg, Manitoba, R3G 0X3.
www.fernwoodpublishing.ca

Fernwood Publishing Company Limited gratefully acknowledges the financial support of the Government of Canada through the Canada Book Fund, the Canada Council for the Arts, the Nova Scotia Department of Tourism and Culture and the Province of Manitoba, through the Book Publishing Tax Credit, for our publishing program.

Library and Archives Canada Cataloguing in Publication
Peshkov-Chow, Ernesto Raj, 1953-
Great multicultural north : a Canadian primer /
Ernesto (Ernie) Raj Peshkov-Chow.
Co-published by Red Publishing.
ISBN 978-1-55266-383-7

1. Multiculturalism--Canada.  2. National characteristics, Canadian.
I. Title.
FC105.M8P47 2010                305.800971
C2010-902940-2

# Contents

# Acknowledgements

I'd like to thank my ancestors, who despite being told they were not quite real Canadians, knew they belonged to this land and that this land belonged to them. My great-great-grandfather Walter Chow, who was born in Barkerville in 1869, the son of a Chinese gold miner from California and a Metis whorehouse owner from Fort St. James deserves special recognition for instilling pride of background into all of his children. Walter was a believer in multiculturalism long before it became fashionable. In 1889 he married the daughter of a freed American slave, who immigrated to Salt Spring Island in the 1850s, and a Hawaiian man, whose family had been brought to North America as indentured servants in the 1840s by the Hudson's Bay Company. In 1910 their first-born son, John Chow, married the daughter of Russian-Finnish anarchists whose son was my grandfather Leo Peshkov-Chow. In 1931 he married Surinder Ghopal and two months later my father Raj was born. Leo was an aircraft mechanic and during World War II joined the RCAF and moved to Moose Jaw where after the war he became a shop teacher. My dad Raj met my mother Julietta Martinez in Moose Jaw in 1949. She was traveling across the country with her father, a Spanish Civil War veteran married to an Arab-Berber born in Morocco, who spoke about Franco and the Canadians who fought in the Mackenzie-Papineau Brigade. And then I came along a few years later.

As a kid I tried to do some mathematical calculation about my ethnicity but gave up because it was too complicated. I decided instead to call myself a Mongrel-Canadian and be proud of it. There are millions like me — the Mongrel Horde — the sons and daughters of all those who were neither English nor French and so were told the bullshit lie that they were not part of Canada's founding people. This book is dedicated to them.

This book is also dedicated to another sort of ancestor — these ones political rather than genetic — all those women and men who believed themselves to be human beings with rights equal to all others, rather than members of some special racial, ethnic, national, religious or political group, and fought for the kind of democracy that reflected this belief. We are not an extinct species. We live on in every corner of the world, despite the temporary triumph of one dollar one vote as the world's dominant governing principle.

I'd also like to thank the union brothers and sisters I have known over the years, first in the IBEW, especially those who survived the Lenkurt Electric strike, which was my first picket line when I was fifteen; then the hundreds of people I met on the Teamsters picket line at Becker's Milk in Toronto; the shop stewards at Steelworkers Local 1005 at Stelco in Hamilton; the activists of the TWU who fought the good fight with B.C. Tel and then the rank and file of the HEU and CUPE who battled the Gordon Campbell provincial government. This book is also for all those brothers and sisters who understand you only get what you're willing to fight for.

Finally, this book owes its existence to Gary Engler, my journalist and union friend. He let me inhabit his brain. I mean, all I really did was talk and he typed. He corrected most of my bad grammar and made me sound funnier and more educated than I really am. He argued with me when I was totally off base and he put up with my bad moods, including my rants, some of which were left in the book, just to give you an idea of what a crabby old bastard I can be. Not many people would spend so much effort expressing the ideas of an ordinary Joe. Not many people would have had the balls to continue talking to me even after I, and everyone like me, supposedly died. This book belongs to both of us. Having said that, I, and I alone, am responsible for all the mistakes, lies, half-truths and swearing that follow.

# Introduction

This is a book for anyone who has ever pondered what it means to be Canadian. Not proud-of-the-pink-bits-on-the-map, stick-it-to-the-Frenchies Canadian, not rich-people-selling-out-to-the-even-richer-American-military-industrial-complex Canadian, not Ottawa-endorsed-sanitized-this-country-can-do-no-wrong-beer-commercial Canadian, but for the new-majority-made-up-of-millions-of-ordinary-people-who-are-part-of-the-thousands-of-minority-communities-that-inhabit-this-land-and-want-to-know-the-truth Canadian.

This is also a book for anyone thinking about becoming Canadian.

This is a book for anyone who cares what a hockey-loving, cranky, working-class-union-guy, Metis-Finnish-Hawaiian-Russian-Chinese-Spanish-Arab-Berber-African-Indo-and-who-knows-what-else-Canadian thinks about his country.

This is a book about a place that could be the most important country in the world. This is a book about how the Canadian circle can accommodate all those who choose to live within it. This is a book about how Canadians can help the world get along despite ethnic and religious differences while building an economy based on need rather than greed that enhances the environment rather than destroying it. This is a book about how Canada can be a model for the entire planet.

This book began as one more attempt to answer the question: "What the hell is a Canadian?" But it quickly became "So, what would Canadians like to be?" and then "What the Boom Boom Geffrion are Canadians becoming?" and "Hey, do we like what we are becoming?" and "If we are becoming more like what we wish to be then why don't we make what we are becoming the essence of what it is we define as being Canadian?" and then finally "Are you sure this new definition of Canadian is something that would piss off the Americans? A little bit, but not so much that they would actually get mad at us."

Sorry if you think I'm making fun of Canadians.

Of course I am. It's what we do.

How do you explain Canada? If you've ever been on the other side of the planet and been asked to describe Canadians and their country, you know how tough it is. You start with the easy stuff, like the weather, the geography, and the famous people. Turns out we are best known for hockey players, actors, singers and comedians. The last one seems to surprise non-Canadians the most. Canada is not perceived to be a funny place, but Canadian humour is, in fact, a serious business. In fact, according to ComCan, a division of the Intellectual Property branch of the Department of Trade, Industry, Commerce, and Digging Deep Holes into the Earth, about 4.16536356% of our Gross Domestic

Product is a direct or indirect result of our sense of humour. At about 8.33072712% of the total population, we produce the highest number of comedians per capita in the world. Of course, because there's more to make fun of and the pay is better in the United States, many of them move south. There they get even funnier because, well, the USA is a pretty funny place, and outsiders see contradictions and anomalies — the building blocks of humour — better than insiders. But our economy does benefit when they return to their roots, building summer mansions in their hometowns of Dildo, Come-by-Chance, Nick's Nose Cove, Snake's Bight, Malignant Cove, Mushaboom, Shag Harbour, Point Prim, Burnt Church, Poodiac, Asbestos, Rivière de Trois Pistoles, Bent River, Pronto, Wawa, Flin Flon, Jackhead, Eyebrow, Elbow, Fertile, Drinkwater, High Level, Legal, Entrance, Bliss Landing, Blubber Bay, Salmon Arm, Snag, Enterprise, Moose Jaw and Climax.

Feeling like outsiders is why Canadians become comedians in the first place. We have always been cultural trespassers trying to fit in, starting with the first Europeans who depended on the wisdom of the First Nations to survive. Then, France, England and the United States defined the culture that we were told we should aspire to. We looked to them, but were not them. Our interloper status is what gives Canadian humour its edge. We're like my great-uncle, a descendent of American slaves who could pass as white. We look like them, we learn to talk like them, so they think we are one of them, but deep down we know who we are. Or, we don't, because we're brought up to believe we should be like them, or at least desire to be like them — whether that was the French or the English or the Americans — but a part of our soul remains true to who we really are, which is not them.

"Not them" has become our defining characteristic. Our core identity is oppositional, a negative, which is perfect for being a Toronto Maple Leaf fan or a comedian or a critic or a writer, because it makes you question everything, but not so good for any sort of self-promotion or even self-defin-ition. On the other hand, building a brand of nationalism based on being "not them" raises interesting possibilities. The result could be a new form of post-ethnic, internationalist nationalism. Our inability to define ourselves could be what defines us as world leaders in the creation of exactly the sort of ideology the planet desperately requires.

Sorry if this is confusing. But we are Canadian and confusion is something we specialize in. And when we are confused we talk about it a lot before we settle on some sort of compromise, then lie about it, later tell jokes about it, then figure out compromise was probably the wisest policy in the first place, then say that's what makes us better than Americans. But the truth is we were confused.

Making fun of ourselves, then apologizing for it, is so Canadian. Or at least we think it might be. Making fun of ourselves, or others, then apologizing for it, then saying, "that is so Canadian," then questioning exactly what that means, is even more Canadian. Making fun of ourselves, or others, then apologizing for it, then saying, "that is so Canadian," then questioning exactly what that means and failing to come up with a consensus, is the most Canadian. In fact, there is almost a consensus among Canadians that there is no consensus among Canadians.

We are a land too big, with too few people sharing any one background and we hate generalizations almost as much as we like telling jokes, so attempting to define the essence of Canada meets with the same success as the Maple Leafs chasing the Stanley Cup. It did happen, a few times, once upon a time, and it's a dream worth cherishing at the beginning of every season. But, given the record, don't bet the family's waterfront property in the Muskokas on the outcome.

The really funny thing is that our diversity and our hopeless lack of consensus could be exactly what the world needs. Our inability to define what it means to be Canadian is, in fact, the essence of a new sort of nationalism, one that is post-ethnic and internationalist.

This book is intended to be both a primer (soft I) and a primer (hard I). It is a short, easy to read (and fun?) explanation of Canada. But, it is also designed to be a small charge that sets off a bigger explosion of a new sort of Canadian nationalism.

You know what I really hate? When an Englishman, especially one with a hoity upper class accent, comes here and starts saying "America this" and "America that" like they bloody well think the term includes Canada. A warning, eh! Canada has only one capital offence in its criminal code: We set afloat on melting Arctic sea ice, with a polar bear, anyone who uses the word "America" to refer to us. The United States annexed that word long ago and made it part of their Manifest Destiny.

# CHAPTER 1

# Canadian?

What is a Canadian? There's some good news and bad news in the answer. First the bad: No one knows. Other than the obvious answer of a Canadian is anyone who is a citizen of Canada. We haven't come up with a good generalization that covers everyone who lives here. We have all sorts of widely accepted stereotypes, depending where you live inside Canada, about the various peoples who make up our country: Ontario WASPs (white Anglo-Saxon Protestants, not the creatures who make their nests under your porch) are uptight, French Canadians are emotional, Newfoundlanders talk funny and … Ottawa Valley talk funny and … Maritimers are lazy and won't take a job far away from home (except for Cape Bretoners who have no choice), Vancouverites are dope smoking, tree-huggers, Albertans wear cowboy hats and have red necks, to mention only a few. But, perhaps due to the paucity of positive images, we have not managed to project one of our internal self images to the outside world, which is what the Americans did with their Yankee entrepreneur. The closest we have come to defining who we are is to vote Tommy Douglas the greatest Canadian ever. He was the long-time socialist premier of Saskatchewan credited with creating Medicare, our universal, government-run health insurance plan. Interestingly, he was also one of the greatest public speakers this country ever produced and very, very funny. And when the greatest Canadian became leader of the federal socialist party he never attracted more than 15% of the vote. So, to sum up, the bad news is we don't know what it means to be Canadian, but we think it has something to do with being socially progressive, funny and not too successful.

The good news is, because no one can answer this question, because we don't know exactly what it means to be Canadian, it doesn't take long before anyone can proclaim himself one of us.

The key words to use are multicultural and tolerant. "I am proud to be part of this great multicultural and tolerant country." Say this and you're in. While we didn't plan for things to be this way — in true Canadian fashion it just happened as a result of compromise over many years — you have to admit there is a certain utility. It means we are inclusive, rather than exclusive. It means we've learned to accept differences better than most. The fact that it also means we're kind of wishy-washy is one of the things we apologize for, but deep down we're proud and prefer to describe it as polite pragmatism.

Of course, there have been attempts over the years to tell us who we are, to "forge a nation" or instill "Canadian" values, but most of us successfully resisted. This is not because we didn't want a national identity, but because the particular one they were trying to shove down our gullets meant giving up who we really were. And while "peace, order and good government" may suit us some of the time, taking orders does not. Throughout our history this sort of thing came from the top down, but we are who we are, not who they tell us to be. When I went to school in the 1950s and early 60s in Moose Jaw, Saskatchewan, for example, we were taught everything English, from history to songs to food. Canadians were supposed to be like them: efficient, war-like, empire builders who were polite and ate boring food. Kids were given a ruler with a list of all the English monarchs on the back so we could cheat on tests that were designed to prove British history was Canadian history. We were also taught real Canadians didn't like garlic or horseradish or any spice except, maybe, a little pepper and salt. The vegetables available in local stores were potatoes, onions, carrots, green cabbage plus canned corn and peas, so vegetarians died off within a month.

Being a Canadian meant you were proud to live in one of the pink bits on the big map at the front of the classroom and, of course, every last French-, Ukrainian-, Scots-, Metis-, Irish-, German-, Polish-, Chinese-, Russian-, Japanese-, Italian-, African-Mongrel-Canadian one of us kids in class were. But no matter how much the school insisted, most of us knew we were not English. Certainly not Orange Order — they were the ones who got the really good jobs with the CPR — because we ate cabbage rolls with garlic sausage or stir-fried vegetables with bok choy from the garden, not Yorkshire pudding. Sure, we'd sing the British Grenadiers and God Save the Queen at school, but when it came to playing war in backyards, some of us always got stuck playing the Krauts or the Japs.

Perhaps that's the key to understanding what a Canadian really is. Since soon after the arrival of Europeans the majority of people on this land were never part of the official idea. When told they were loyal members of some great Protestant English empire, too many of them were First Nations or French or Catholic. Then, by the time official Canada changed course and said the country had two founding peoples, French and English, too many of us were eastern European or Italian, or Chinese or south Asian, or First Nation, or Chilean, or Metis, or Armenian, or Sudanese, or Lebanese, or from a hundred other places.

A "multicultural society" is the one idea that seems to reflect our on-the-ground reality, but what does that mean for building a nation and our nationalism? We're a people with so many pasts, that it's hard to define a single present. We're much too complicated for a simple generalization about who we are. Rather, we're a possibility, so far unrealized, based upon compromise, a desire to get along and a sense of humour. We are what happens when people come together from all over the world and learn to live together more or less peacefully, sharing their common humanity and building something not quite finished yet. Plus we're definitely not American.

Of course that doesn't help very much in our quest to define who we are. So, in good Canadian fashion, to come up with an answer we'll avoid the question, at least for now, and instead take a look at some of the less controversial stuff about this country.

One thing everyone can agree on is Canada has a lot of land, so let's start there. Canada is the second biggest country in the world, by area, yet most of us crowd together in big cities in a narrow southern strip near the border with the USA. This is not because we want to be close to Americans, but rather the weather usually gets better the further south you go. In fact, Canada exists because Americans didn't want the cold bits of North America enough to fight another war against England. (That's why global warming and Britain's current best-buddy status with the USA worries some of us so much.)

Our 33.93 million people (early 2010 estimate), making us the 35th most populous country in the world, occupy just less than nine million square kilometres of land and we have another million of water to canoe in during summer and skate on in winter. If you look at the country as a whole there are 3.5 people per square kilometre (The United States has 31 people/km2, France 109 and the United Kingdom 246), but if you look at where over 80% of us live, in urban areas, the density averages 245 people /km2. Canada is one of the most urban countries in the world, despite, or maybe because of, all that land. Forty-five per cent of us live in six cities with more than one million people: Toronto, Montréal, Vancouver, Ottawa, Calgary and Edmonton. Those six cities are also growing faster than anywhere else.

We like the empty spaces; we just don't want to live there. We've discovered that if you get a million or more people in close proximity you generate enough heat to reduce the amount of snow that falls each winter.

Weather is a big deal in Canada. In fact, the most successful non English- or French-speaking immigrants are the ones who quickly learn the words to say how hot or cold or windy or humid or rainy or snowy it is today. They fit right in sitting in a Tim Horton's coffee shop complaining about the weather. Some people think we want new Canadians who are trained physicians, or engineers, or nurses, or carpenters — and sure we probably do — but all that foreign higher education and experience doesn't mean a damn thing unless you can describe the size of the hail that just caused $2,500 damage on your brand new built-in-Alliston-Ontario Honda. And then blame the government, preferably in both official languages.

Which brings up the delicate subject of politics. (So much for staying with stuff that we all agree on.)

Canada is made up of 10 provinces and three territories (which are not quite provinces because too few people live there). There's a federal government in Ottawa that makes laws about some stuff and provincial and territorial governments that set the rules on other things. Which government does what can get confusing because, while there was a list in the British North America Act that set up Canada in 1867, nowadays there are many overlapping jurisdictions due to the principle of he who owns the credit card orders the iTune.

For example, health and education are provincial responsibilities according to the BNA Act, but Ottawa pays for a lot of these programs so it gets to make some rules and generally stick its nose into other people's affairs and royally piss off provincial governments, especially when an election is near.

The prime minister, almost always the leader of the party that wins the most seats in the House of Commons, runs the government. Only the Liberals and Conservatives have ever formed federal governments, of which there are two kinds, majority or minority. With a majority government the prime minister has more power than a president in a typical republic, but a little less than a Roman emperor. In a minority government, where no one party gets a majority of seats, the prime minister governs a little more carefully, because he usually wants to avoid a new election, which is called when the government loses a vote of confidence. (This is not where the term "confidence man" comes from, or at least I don't think so.) Who would have guessed, but it seems that as soon as a politician gets an office in Ottawa, he'd rather not have another election, unless he thinks he's going to win again or his term is up. Some say a minority government is more democratic because it reflects the divided political loyalties of Canadians, but most of us don't like them because the one thing we hate more than having a party we don't like in power is having a party we don't like in power that we can't really blame because they only have a minority.

There are currently 308 seats in the House of Commons, each representing a riding (also called a constituency) that is a specified part of the country. In each riding we have what is commonly called a first-past-the-post election. This means each candidate is like a horse in a race and the first one to get past the finish line is the winner. Doesn't matter how many horses there are, only one can win. (Of course, the more horses in the race, the more horseshit there will be on the track to clean up afterwards.)

In theory, in a democracy, each riding should have more or less the same number of voters, right? Forget about that in the Canadian system. The average Prince Edward Island riding has 34,000 residents, while the average Newfoundland riding has 72,140, New Brunswick 73,000, Nova Scotia 83,000, Québec 100,610, Ontario 114,700, Manitoba 82,000, Saskatchewan 69,140, Alberta 117,500, and B.C. 114,250. They say these big differences are because no province can have fewer members of parliament than it has senators. But, then to further put the kibosh to the principle of one person, one vote, we have this unspoken rule that one farmer equals at least two city dwellers in terms of voting power. I've never been able to get a satisfactory explanation for this, but best I understand, the reasons are something like: Farmers got to drive farther and use up more gas to get to the polling place so we got to make it worth their while by at least doubling their voting power. Or farmers are at least twice as smart as city guys, because they can only get CBC on the radio when they're out on the back forty driving the tractor. Or the electoral commission thinks it looks bad when the city ridings are tiny dots on a map and the rural ridings cover half a province. The bottom line is that urban ridings have one hell of a lot more voters than rural — over 150,000 compared to around 30,000. Strange things can happen as a result. For example, a Conservative candidate in a Vancouver riding could get 15,000 votes, yet come in third, while a Liberal candidate in Prince Edward Island who gets 12,000 votes wins his seat. Or 15% of the people across Alberta vote NDP and 25% vote Liberal, but only Conservatives get elected from the province.

Of course we do have a Charter of Rights and Freedoms in Canada that says: "Every individual is equal before and under the law and has the right to the equal protection and equal benefit of the law without discrimination ..." so, in theory, someone could go to the supreme court and argue this whole election process is unconstitutional on the grounds an individual in PEI and an individual in Alberta are, in fact, not equal when it comes to their vote and perhaps they'd win their case. But ... We are so fond of buts in Canada that we even have one in our Charter of Rights and Freedoms. It's commonly called the "notwithstanding clause" and it says the federal or provincial governments can, in fact, pass some laws that go against the Charter if they really, really, really, really want to. They'd look bad, of course, which is no small thing, but they could do it.

Don't misunderstand, the Charter is an important document, with all sorts of good things in it, and tells you a lot about Canada. For example, there is a section that says the "Charter shall be interpreted in a manner consistent with the preservation and enhancement of the multicultural heritage of Canadians." How many other countries have such a clause? Or how about a country whose charter of rights has eight of a total 34 sections dealing with language and associated rights? There are more words about language and associated rights in the Charter than about legal rights. What does that say about us? We are a nation obsessed with the subject and discuss it endlessly in at least two official languages. The funny thing is that an obvious solution is one thing almost never talked about. If we passed a law that said everyone who went to school had to become fluent in, at least, both English and French, everybody would be fully bilingual within a generation or two. The two languages might even merge into one new one — like some people in Montréal already talk — and we'd all speak Canadian. We don't talk about this because a dislike of bilingualism is one thing both Québec nationalists and Québec haters agree on.

Instead, we have reached a more or less happy compromise that goes like this: Most people in Québec, outside of some parts of Montréal, learn French only, while most people in the rest of Canada learn English only. People in some parts of the Maritimes, western Québec and eastern Ontario learn both languages so they can get jobs with the federal government. And then there's the better educated and upwardly mobile French and English across the country who make sure their children speak both official languages just in case they want to run for prime minister or be appointed to run some federal department or Crown corporation. This state of affairs seems to be working and in good Canadian fashion, we may make jokes about it, but we do not fix things until they are really, really broken. Otherwise another constitutional crisis could break out.

Of all the strange things about our federal government the strangest involve this thing we call the Senate. It's the other place on Parliament Hill, in Ottawa, next door to the House of Commons, the elected part of our federal government. The senators are appointed by whatever government is in place when a spot comes open, which once was upon death, but now there's mandatory retirement, even though the government has abolished that in most other jobs. But the government can't just pick anybody to replace a dead or retired senator. They have to follow the formula that was written into the BNA Act in 1867. Some say the idea was to give 24 seats in the Senate to each region, but I think the best way to understand how it works is that some provinces bargained harder than others, and got a better deal. Québec and Ontario are each guaranteed 24 spots in the Senate, while the same number goes to the West and Atlantic regions.

Sounds fair, right? Except that Newfoundland isn't considered part of the Atlantic region because it didn't join the country until 1949 and it was given its own six senators. That means New Brunswick and Nova Scotia each get 10 while Prince Edward Island, the smallest province in both area and population, gets four. So, the smallest four provinces, with a combined population of 2,284,000 (in 2006) get 30 senators, while Ontario with 12,160,000 people and Québec with 7,546,000 also each get 24. And that's not the worst of it. The four western provinces get screwed the most, with Manitoba (1,148,000 people), Saskatchewan (968,000), Alberta (3,290,000) and British Columbia (4,113,000) each getting six senate seats. Go west young man, unless you want to be a senator.

In most countries something so unfair as this might cause a revolution, or at minimum, fill a large hall with a lot of guys yelling. But, in typical Canadian style, we have a more creative solution.

Few people care much about how rotten and unrepresentative the Senate is, because we don't give it any power. They say the Senate is the chamber of sober second thought, which seems to be a backhanded insult about the drinking habits of the honourable members who sit in the House of Commons, but apparently isn't. It's just another way of saying a bunch of old wise guys (not the ones from New Jersey) get together after a bill has been passed in the House of Commons and talk about it. Every once in a while they come up with an idea nobody thought about before and actually earn their pay by improving a bill before it becomes law. But, other than being an advisory board, they can't do much. Certainly not like the wise guys in the Godfather movies who can decide who wakes up with a horse's head beside them under the sheets.

Truth is you need to pay attention to Canadian politics a long time to figure out all the parts of government that don't have any real power. Like our supposed equivalent of president, our head of state, is the Queen (or King) of England. But, she has no power, except to appoint her representative, which she doesn't do because it's the prime minister who chooses the governor general. And the governor general also has no real power. She (women from the media have been a popular choice in the last decade) mostly just meets people and has her picture taken a lot. This kind of government is so popular that each province also has a celebrity head of state, called the lieutenant governor.

But don't get the wrong idea; I'm not making fun of our government. Nothing above should in any way be taken to mean that Canadians dislike government. We do like it, sort of. We do because that's one of the things that makes us different from our neighbours to the south. Governments have given us lots of things for the common good, such as Medicare and the CBC and the CRTC ruling that made our radio stations play Celine Dion, Bryan Adams, Sarah McLachlan, Nickelback, k.d. lang, Barenaked Ladies, Avril Lavigne, Diana Krall, Rush, Alanis Morissette, Trooper, Nelly Furtado, Shania Twain and Michael Bublé to name but a few of hundreds of Canadians who have infiltrated the world music charts. Before the government's Canadian content ruling few singers from this country got played on the radio. The best that most Canadian singers could hope for back then was to become a lounge act in Las Vegas.

Of course you'd have a hard time saying what Canadian music is, other than defining it as stuff Canadians do. Which is a lot like asking the more general question: What is a Canadian? (I told you'd we'd get to that.)

We've always been so much better at defining what we're not than what we are. Perhaps that's where to look to help define what is a Canadian.

You know what really pisses me off? How the bigwigs and their ass-kissers in the media, the pro-Americans and the neoliberalcons lie to us and some people actually believe them. And they don't tell little white lies, they tell big whoppers. You know the sort: Up is down, war is peace, socialized medicine is bad for your health, raising the minimum wage hurts poor people, the U.S. fights for freedom around the world, unions aren't needed any more, build more freeways to get rid of traffic jams... When you get me on a really grumpy day I'd probably tell you that the whole bloody U.S. capitalist system is an illusion promoted by lies, maintained by police and armies, designed to make one per cent or less of the population really, really rich.

CHAPTER **2**

# What we're not

Anyone who walks through media pastures knows bullshit is everywhere, fresh and steaming, but also old and dried out. These are called myths. While that sort of poop is great as a fertilizer, it's generally not a good idea to rely on it directly for nourishment. Still, the lies we tell about ourselves reveal who we are almost as much as the truth.

As a place with long periods of crappy weather where people hang out together in close quarters to survive the snow or rain, the inhabitants of this land have always been bullshitters. Which is just a less polite way of saying that we're an oral people and storytelling is a good way to pass the time when it's hard to get out.

While we've been less successful at making the world swallow Canadian cow pies than our neighbours to the south, we've been pretty good purveyors of tall tales and myths. Like most of these sorts of stories, ours tell us a lot about the character of the people who created them. They reveal Canada's collective aspirations. Still, it's best to tread carefully through fields where you can get stuck knee-deep in steaming piles of folklore.

Let's examine some of our most common myths and see what they tell us about us.

**Myth 1: Canadians are peaceful and respect authority**

How we came to believe this about ourselves is a mystery, when hockey is our most popular sport and lacrosse is our second official national game. Anybody who has witnessed a junior hockey game, or even better, a junior lacrosse game, knows that Canadians are an aggressive, violence-loving people who hate and ridicule the upholders of law and order. There are thousands of arenas across the country where, every night from September through April, you can witness Canadians cheering wildly for their side in a fistfight and mocking the referee who misses a penalty against the other team, or worse, calls a bad one against our side. Visit George Street in St. John's or Electric Avenue in Calgary or Granville Street in Vancouver to see how well Canadians respect police officers around closing time of the many bars in these "entertainment" districts. Blame the Mounties, the Klondike gold rush and Walt Disney for this myth. According to the movies a lone Northwest Mounted Police officer whipped all those American prospectors into shape and he did it without once using his gun. This became the founding mythology of Canada's national police force because it made a much better story than the reality of the first big operation of the Mounties, which was crushing the Metis and First Nations rebellion of 1885, then arresting and hanging Louis Riel. It's tough to glorify the hangmen of a Canadian icon. Much easier to laugh at cartoons of Dudley Do-right and enjoy the Musical Ride. The truth is, while most Canadians value peace, order and good government and think handguns are dangerous, we still enjoy a good fight and know who among us aspire to become cops: Many good people and some guys who crave power. Sure the Mounties with lances up there on the horses look good, but the ones who set fire to the Québec barn and shot dead the strikers in Estevan in 1931 were not so pretty. And the cops who Tasered to death a Polish immigrant they found guilty of not speaking English and hanging around too long in the Vancouver Airport waiting room just proved the point again.

## Myth 2: Canadians are either French or English

This is the oldest myth of all, the basis of which was the centuries-long France-England rivalry for economic and political control over much of what is now Canada. But, there never was a time when people descended from inhabitants of France or England were the majority in what is now Canada. To fall for this story you must believe First Nations did not exist, that Irish, Scots and Welsh are, in fact, English, and that the millions of Germans, Italians, Poles, Ukrainians, Hungarians, Dutch, Finns, Norwegians, Swedes, Ibo, Tutsis, Indians, Chinese, and others can be defined solely by the language that comes out of their subsequent generations' mouths. Millions of us grew up through the 1960s learning about the pink bits on the world map and although I may be an English-speaking Canadian, I never was an English-Canadian. People descended from inhabitants of France who immigrated to Canada are the largest single group currently living in this country, followed by people from England, Scotland, Ireland and Germany. But the most important point is that none of these ethnic backgrounds claims anywhere near a majority of today's 33 million Canadians.

The official data from the 2006 census (population 31.6 million) in which people checked off one or more ethnic origins has:

| | |
|---|---|
| Canadian | 10.1 million* |
| English | 6.6 million |
| French | 4.9 million |
| Scottish | 4.7 million |
| Irish | 4.4 million |
| German | 3.2 million |
| Aboriginal | 1.7 million |
| Italian | 1.4 million |
| Chinese | 1.3 million |
| Ukrainian | 1.2 million |
| Dutch | 1.0 million |

*According to Statistics Canada, people of French background are the most likely to choose Canadian as an ethnic category.*

The list of ethnic backgrounds included over 200 different responses. Over 41% of the population reported more than one ethnic background. Someone like me, who has ancestors who were (just the ones I know about) Metis, Chinese, Hawaiian, African, Russian, Indian, Spanish, Arab and Berber will soon be the norm. The lingering remnants of the United Empire Loyalists and the Orange Order may find it comforting to define all who speak English as English-Canadians. The ultra-nationalists in Québec may find utility in stirring up fears about a growing English-Canadian threat. But, the biggest chunk of us prefer to be just plain Canadians.

So why does this myth persist? Perhaps because it simplifies things and the best myths are easy to understand. It gives us a history, about perseverance, accommodation and getting along, which we find useful. Then there's the French-English tension that keeps us on our toes. Feeling content, on top of the world and the centre of the universe produces U.S. foreign policy and the Toronto Maple Leafs. It's better to always feel a little unstable, a little the underdog, to dance the two-language tango and keep a slight chip on your shoulder like the Canadiens, who have won the most Stanley Cups.

Call it our two solitudes, call it the Canadian dialectic, call it social schizophrenia — it's an important part of who we are.

## Myth 3: Canada is a bilingual country

The country is sometimes promoted with an image of sophisticated, Pierre Trudeau-like characters, effortlessly switching between French and English, but the truth is much different. In our dreams Canadians speak French and English, but in reality less than one in five of us can communicate in both official languages. (According to the 2006 census, 42.4% of francophones report being able to conduct a conversation in both English and French versus 9.4% of anglophones.) Many of us speak neither language at home. In fact, census data show we're rather complicated linguistically.

**Language spoken most often at home**

| | |
|---|---|
| English | 20,584,775 |
| French | 6,608,120 |
| Other | 3,472,130 |

**Top-25 Canadian Mother Tongues**

| | |
|---|---|
| English | 18,232,200 |
| French | 6,970,405 |
| Italian | 476,905 |
| Chinese | 467,235 |
| German | 466,655 |
| Punjabi | 382,585 |
| Cantonese | 369,645 |
| Spanish | 362,120 |
| Arabic | 286,790 |
| Tagalog (Filipino) | 266,445 |
| Portuguese | 229,280 |
| Polish | 217,605 |
| Mandarin | 173,730 |
| Urdu | 156,420 |
| Vietnamese | 146,410 |
| Ukrainian | 141,805 |
| Persian | 138,075 |
| Russian | 136,235 |
| Dutch | 133,240 |
| Korean | 128,120 |
| Greek | 123,575 |
| Tamil | 122,020 |
| Gujarati | 86,285 |
| Hindi | 85,500 |
| Cree | 84,905 |

Most of us think bilingualism is good for the country, but it's too much work for me. Anyone who lives in a car-dominated culture can relate because it's kind of like driving instead of walking to the corner store to pick up a carton of milk — you do what's easiest, not what's best for you. In most parts of Canada, there's not much need, or incentive, to become bilingual, because one language dominates. On the other hand, in the places where bilingualism offers jobs or business opportunities, many people do make the effort. Which is really just a long-winded way of saying French-speaking people are much more likely to learn English than the other way around. Knowing English opens up the possibility of living and working in Vancouver, Calgary and Los Angeles for a unilingual French speaker. Knowing French opens up the possibility of living and working in Chibougamau, Chicoutimi and Québec City for a unilingual English speaker. So, in Montréal, a business centre where most of the best jobs require a working knowledge of French and English, 52% of the population was bilingual in 2006. In Ottawa, where to get ahead in the civil service one needs to speak both official languages, just over 44% of the population was bilingual in 2006. Compare that to Toronto, where French is irrelevant for work anywhere but in some government jobs and only 8.25% of the population was bilingual, or 7.75% in Vancouver, where speaking French is pretty much only done at home or in some of the finest restaurants. Canadians do what is practical.

Sure, if it were easy, most of us would be bilingual. We prefer the urbane bilingual world traveler as an ideal over that of the ignorant American who thinks if he just speaks loud enough everyone will understand him. While we may be lazy, at least we aspire to be better than we are.

## Myth 4: Canada is a land of snow

We love snow, sort of. Most of us grow up playing in it, making snow angels, snowmen, snow castles, snow forts, snow tunnels and have snowball fights. We ski on it. We snowshoe. We eat it. We paint its vast vistas. We long for it when the heat and humidity of August become unbearable. We are snow people.

But, like any sensible snow people we also hate it. Many of us try to avoid the snow by moving to Vancouver and Vancouver Island, or by spending the winter in Florida, Arizona or Hawaii.

The real reason there are so many pro-American Canadians is that the Yanks have winter escapes. Snowbirds are the USA's fifth column in Canada.

The real motivation for the Monroe Doctrine was to keep British North America from the warm bits south of the USA. And it's easy to guess why we release more greenhouse gases per capita than any other place on the planet: For us the idea of global warming has a definite attraction. Still, we do like the idea of being in tune with the land and the environment, including snow. After all, it is pretty. If it just didn't take so much energy to shovel it, if it didn't fall, then melt, then freeze into an endless series of traps for our favourite aunts to breaks their hips, if it didn't start in October and end in April ...

## Myth 5: Canada is a force for good in world affairs

This is often linked with the notion that we are a peaceful people, which, in international affairs, is even more absurd than the idea we all get along inside our own country. Sure, we'd like to be a force for good in the world, but who would answer "no" if asked that? If they did polling in Nazi Germany, the majority of people would likely have said their country was a force for good in the world. This is a myth useful to governments in the same way beer company ads try to convince young men that its brand will help them pick up women. Drink lots of beer and the ladies will fall for you. Reality is far from the message, but sex does sell. "We are a force for good in the world" is the message governments use to help sell foreign policy that, if understood clearly, would be unpalatable to many citizens. Honestly, what is Canada's record in world affairs? Certainly from 1867 until 1945 we were not much more than a few fingers at the end of one of Britain's long arms. Canadian troops fought in the Boer War in South Africa, in World War I, in the intervention against the Red Army after the Russian Revolution and in World War II, all under British command, or at least direction. Our foreign policy, such as one existed, was more or less British foreign policy. So, in order for Canada to be seen as a force for good in the world during this period, one would have to argue that the British Empire was a force for good in the world. Billions of people in Asia, Africa, the Caribbean and the Middle East would disagree, not to mention European and American rivals for imperial power. But what about after World War II, when supposedly, as our story goes, we began to focus on peacekeeping and developed an independent foreign policy? Unfortunately in this period too our collective aspiration seldom corresponded to reality.

There is no doubt that the vast majority of Canadians want our country to be a force for good in the world, to keep peace rather than be a junior imperial power, to have an independent foreign policy. But wanting does not make it so. The truth is our elites have always sided with whatever country or empire was the most powerful. The facts speak for themselves. You can read hundreds of academic papers and books that demonstrate Canadian foreign policy since World War II has primarily been focused on being a junior partner to the USA. Our military has become a branch of their military even though the only conceivable realistic enemy we have is the USA. What really irks Canadian neoconservatives, who understand how pro-American our foreign policy has been, is that most of us prefer to believe the myth of Canada as peacekeeper. The neo-cons want us to face up to our reality, and more, to like it. But even millions of Americans don't like their country's foreign policy, so why should we? And our generations-old instinct is to mistrust their motives. After all, the one country ever to invade our territory was the USA. Most of us think it wise to be friendly with our cousins across the line. Like the middle-aged couple who live next door, we'll share the cost of a fence, we'll cut the lawn when they go on holidays and they're welcome to drop over for a visit anytime, but we're not interested in sleeping with them.

## Myth 6: People around the world love us

Americans stitch Canadian flags on their backpacks to fool foreigners and make their travels safer, because everyone loves the Great White North. At least that's what we like to believe. Americans pretending to not be who they are while traveling is certainly plausible and that they sometimes pose as Canadians is also believable, but leaping from that to arguing everyone likes us is, at best, naïve. Much more likely is that a Toronto accent is easier to master for the typical American than one from Liverpool, or Auckland, or Cape Town or Melbourne. The truth is most people around the world have no opinion about Canada, so pretending to be one of us is a lot safer that admitting to be an American. Since most Canadians don't know how close we work with the USA in military and foreign affairs, it's not surprising the rest of the world is also ignorant. This is yet another myth that tells more about our relationship with the United States than it does about Canadians. Nah, nah, nah, nah, we're not as bad as you are! You are ugly Americans and we're nice Canadians. We love thinking that. Even after we join in on the latest American hair-brained imperial adventure and some Canadian-owned mining company destroys the water supply of yet another Third World town.

## Myth 7: Canadians are friendly and polite

Strange myth this, because in my experience we are no more, nor less, polite or friendly than people in the dozen, or so, countries to which I have traveled. Our big cities can be just as cold and rude as any on the planet while our small towns are filled with people who smile at strangers and want to know your name. Sure, we say sorry out of reflex, but that is as much self-deprecation as politeness. My theory is that this idea comes from Americans who visit Canada and find we treat them with respect, kindness and just a little fear. This is really because we're nervous they might be packing heat and with our tougher gun control laws, we're at a serious disadvantage so we figure it's wise to treat them right. We're not polite; we're scared of them.

## Myth 8: In Canada religion and ethnicity don't matter

While this may be closer to the truth than in most countries, there are still plenty of racists, bigots and intolerant zealots roaming our land. And remnants of our Orange Order, United Empire Loyalist more-British-than-thou, anti-French, Catholic-versus-Protestant past linger on. For example the places where there's the highest percentage of Protestants are still more likely to vote Conservative. Throughout Canada's history, Catholics were most likely to vote Liberal (or NDP or another third party) and Protestants cast their ballots for Conservative (or NDP or another third party). Like all generalizations it does not always hold true, but if you compare census data regarding religion and voting in federal elections, there is definitely a pattern that continues to this day. Since 43.2% of us describe ourselves as Catholic and 29.2% Protestant (in the 2001 census) this lingering connection between religion and politics goes a long way to explaining why the Liberals have been the "natural governing party" of Canada. (On the other hand, the category of "no religion" at 16.2% is in fact the second largest "denomination" in the country, way ahead of United Church (9.6%), Anglican (6.9%), Baptist (2.5%) Lutheran (2.0%), Muslim (2.0%), Presbyterian (1.4%), Jewish (1.1%), Buddhist (1.0%) Hindu (1.0%), Sikh (0.9%).) Of course, we hardly talk about religion in polite company and most people who claim a denomination seldom attend church. Still, with so many activists in the Conservative Party coming from small evangelical Protestant churches, sooner or later there will be a backlash from the non- and semi-religious and the Catholics. Unlike the United States, here the safest position for politicians is to keep their religion to themselves.

As for equality of ethnic groups and the amount of racism, Canada also falls short of its self-image. Many Canadians, probably most, still think there is something called "race" even though no one can define it. Even worse, many of us still make ignorant generalizations such as the French are like this, the English are like that, Blacks do this, Jews do that, Hindus always ..., Native Indians can't ... etc... The funny thing about these sorts of generalization is that they are only made about people we don't really know. Could you imagine comments such as all my uncles, aunts, cousins, grandparents think they can get away with living on welfare, or everyone on my block is high-strung or people who attend my church are likely to join gangs? The good thing about Canada, and what makes it less racist than many places in the world, is that we have reached the point where everyone is a member of a minority. There is no longer one dominant religion, or ethnic group, or place of origin, or even language in parts of our biggest cities. Some people view this as a problem, but for many of us it is a strength. We like the idea that to be Canadian is to be everyone on the planet. We want our "nationalism" to be internationalism and our "religion" to include the belief that human beings, all living things and the entire planet are interconnected.

## Myth 9: Canada is socialist with great social programs

This myth was definitely made in the USA even though some Canadians also believe it. It's only true if you believe, like some market-worshipping sycophants of the rich and powerful, that all (non-military) government activity is socialist and illegitimate. The truth is Canada is near the bottom of the pack in terms of government-mandated childcare, parental leave, pensions, vacations, minimum wage, unemployment insurance and other social programs, when compared with other industrialized countries. Often the only rich country that is worse is the USA. As for other criteria of judging whether a country is best described as socialist, our governments own very little of the economy and there are very few pictures of Karl Marx around Canada. (Of course there is the awkward fact that we voted the socialist Tommy Douglas the greatest Canadian ever, but let's not linger there.) By one count there were 17 Canadian billionaires in 2007 and north of the border there are no estate taxes, which means the ultra-rich can more easily create aristocracies of wealth than their U.S. counterparts. Some of us wish we were socialist, but the picture of Tommy Douglas is not yet on any denomination of Canada's currency.

So what do our myths tell us about ourselves? That we're all part-time politicians, which is just a cruel way of saying we're sometime liars. But that could be said of every nation around the world. Ultimately, the truth of our self-image is less important than what we choose to delude ourselves with. Whether or not it's true, the fact we prefer to see ourselves as peace-loving, law-abiding, accommodating-of-minorities, in-tune-with-the-environment, sophisticated, bilingual French and English socialists tells us something about ourselves.

But it still doesn't provide a response to: What is a Canadian? We're still missing some pieces of the puzzle. One is our history.

Maybe the people who believe the neocon lies piss me off even more than the liars themselves. I mean how hard is it to educate yourself, at least a little bit? How difficult is it to think for yourself, at least a couple of times a week? Read a book. Google a controversial subject and make sure you consider all sides of the question. Think about alternatives. Take responsibility for learning how you're being screwed. If you can't do that why the hell should we feel sympathy when you start screaming because rich guys are using their power tools to drive sharp metal objects through your wallet and various parts of your body?

# CHAPTER 3

# A short history of Canada

Success on the attack is often determined by how you set up the play behind your net. You can't tell where you're going unless you know where you have been. Understanding our past can tell us a lot about the possibilities of our future.

Some say Canadian history is boring because we've had no revolutionary or civil wars. Instead we had a few minor outbreaks of violence followed by government reports, some legislative reforms and a CBC mini-series, a little later. Our violent outbursts have been short, like our summers, and perhaps the two go together. Make love, not war, makes special sense when a blizzard is raging outside. Plus we've witnessed, up close, militarism and violence south of the border. So, we prefer our fighting in hockey games. (Where most of the combatants' energy is used up pulling each other's equipment off, or smacking their hands against hard plastic. Call it stupid, or homoerotic, but at least we use up our testosterone without bombing cities or invading small countries.) Compromise, rather than confrontation is the most common theme in Canadian history.

Of course there was violence when Europeans claimed First Nations' land. It was the inevitable result of foreigners with a really bad attitude crashing the territory now called

Canada. "Hello stranger, can you help us out? And oh by the way, we claim this land in the name of the King/Queen of France/England." Kind of like if kids from across town show up and say "this street belongs to us and from now on we make the road hockey rules." Every red-blooded Canadian would be prepared for a five-minute fighting major and a game misconduct to stop that. And what would happen today if a few hundred immigrants came on a boat from Nigeria and claimed all of Nova Scotia in the name of the King of the Ibos? They'd be locked up and deported faster than you can say Stephen Harper, Michael Ignatieff, Gilles Duceppe and Jack Layton.

Despite the colonial attitude of the Europeans, including the English, First Nations saved British North America during the American Revolution and then again in the War of 1812. To this day you find First Nation settlements strategically placed to defend Montréal, Kingston, Toronto and other central-Canadian cities against attack from the USA. They defended Canada, made our homes safe, helped some of us get rich, and taught us lacrosse. And what did they get out of it? A crosscheck to the face and a shove to the ground. Okay, they don't have to pay income tax if they live on a reserve where there are no jobs. Plus they can sell cheap cigarettes, now that hardly anyone is smoking. A fair trade for all of the land we stole from them? But, we did it slowly, steadily, peacefully, with compromise (mostly on the First Nations side), in the Canadian way.

The European conquest of Canada was less violent than in many places in the western hemisphere, mostly thanks to the attitude of this land's original inhabitants and to the balance of power among the First Nations and European powers. Most First Nations — about two million people on the land we now call Canada at the time of European contact, speaking over 100 languages — had an attitude of accepting newcomers into their circle. They also had a way of dealing with enemies that was much different than the European idea of conquering. Rather than beating their opponent, competing groups sought relationships with ongoing negotiation in which both sides had to be comfortable — compromise, rather than conquest. Because of the relative strength of First Nations in the land that became Canada, Europeans had to adapt to their ways in order to be successful. For centuries the French and the British needed their alliances with various First Nations to survive and to collect furs, the basis of the European economy in what is now Canada.

The first Europeans that we know about, the Vikings, came to Newfoundland and Labrador about a thousand years ago. These guys didn't last very long because they were poor houseguests, with very bad manners, and outwore their welcome with the original Newfoundlanders. The next recorded contact was also in Newfoundland in the late 1400s when Basque, English, Portuguese and French cod fishing boats began using the many sheltered bays for provisioning. That began the long battle, mostly between French and English merchants, over control of the fishing and fur trade along the north Atlantic coast and into the St. Lawrence River.

Of course, the real go-getter, Bill-Gates types of their day never came here, because the big money was down south in the sugar, tobacco and cotton rackets. Wealth earned from fish and beaver pelts was nothing compared to the huge fortunes — the dotcom boom of its day— that were made from the slavery plantations that extended from Maryland to Brazil. Trafficking in human beings to grow new products for the world market turned out to be very, very profitable. But, while Newfoundland salt cod fed slaves, Canada mostly watched the riches pile up in other parts of the world. We may have missed out on the big money, but we also avoided the legacy of large-scale slavery that fouls the USA, Caribbean and many South American countries to this day.

The French were the first to send over colonists, beginning in the 1600s. A few thousand settled in the St. Lawrence valley and in what would later become the Maritime provinces and Newfoundland. For a century the French built alliances with First Nations that allowed them to expand their trade, primarily in furs, deep into the continent. The English did the same from settlements in New York and New England. Often the First Nations played the two European rivals against each other. While, from the First Nations point of view, the land belonged to them, the two European powers fought each other constantly, with various treaties ceding control of parts of North America from one to the other. One of these treaties gave the English control over what are now Nova Scotia, New Brunswick and Prince Edward Island and in 1755 most French-speakers were expelled. Some of the Acadians ended up in Louisiana where they invented Cajun food and le bon temps Zydeco music. Others came back to Canada, where to this day, they throw the biggest and best family reunions in the world.

At about the time of the Acadian expulsion, the French and English fought in the real first world war, called the Seven Years War, which is known in the United States as the French and Indian War. This resulted in the defeat and withdrawal of the French army and government structure from most of North America. Of course, while many of the officers and some wealthy people returned to France, by this time most ordinary French-speakers had lived in Canada for a hundred years and could not easily leave. Therefore, they had to learn to live with the haggis, mushy peas and potato-eating crowd, the redcoats and his majesty, the Lord Dalyrimple of Worcestershire Sauce, sent over to make the colony right.

The period from the English conquest and the end of the Seven Years War in 1763 through to the aftermath of the American Revolution and the War of 1812 ultimately determined, first, that there would be a Canada; second, that the Canadiens-Maple Leafs rivalry would be a very big deal; and third, that we sing O Canada, not the Star Spangled Banner, because of the First Nations who preferred a border to protect them against the USA.

The truth is Canada came very close to not existing. One of the causes of the American Revolution was that the British were too often, in the eyes of the Americans, upholding treaties and other agreements made with First Nations. The Americans wanted Indian land to expand, but the British sometimes took their previous promises seriously, thus slowing down the expansion of settlements. So, during the revolution, many of the First Nations sided with the British against the Americans. This support, plus the French-speaking population's attitude of "better the maudit Anglais you know than the ones you don't," proved decisive in keeping what is now Québec and Ontario in British hands.

This brings up the biggest difference between American and Canadian narratives of our shared history. In English-speaking Canada, the aftermath of the American Revolution is the time of our country's founding and the source of our existence as "not American." In the USA, the story goes something like this: The War of Independence was fought to free the people from British domination and create a new country with a constitution and a form of government that was a beacon to the world. The war and its aftermath was a time when the new nation was forged. The big, bad British had a hard time letting go and were constantly harassing the new United States of America on the sea and in the west. The British did this because they were vindictive and worried about the glorious example of the USA to the rest of the world. Down south, there is almost never a mention of the people who left the new USA after the revolution, but in Canada these 70,000 United Empire Loyalists are considered the founders of Nova Scotia, New Brunswick, Prince Edward Island and Ontario. They included thousands of aboriginals, most prominently from the Six Nations, who were expelled from the new USA and settled north of the border. As well, thousands of African-Americans who sided with the British were promised land in Canada. While the commitment was only partially honoured, Canada's oldest Black communities, near Halifax, are the descendents of those Loyalists.

The United Empire Loyalists defined Canadian as, first of all, loyal to the Crown, but also as better than American. Some were snooty, aristocratic types, (only a small minority were English — many more were German, Irish, Scots, Dutch, First Nations and Black) and they brought feelings of superiority, a fear of anarchy and a disdain for the crass capitalism found south of the border. From the beginning, there was a strain of Canadian conservatism that featured an aristocratic noblesse oblige and was anti-American. Of course these snooty ultra-English tried to run everything, claiming to be the Canadian aristocracy, so if you wanted to be part of the early Canadian ruling class, but weren't a Loyalist, you joined the Orange Order, an ultra-Protestant, ultra-pro-British organization that was imported from Ireland. It became a way for non-Loyalist immigrants to "out-loyal" the Loyalists, by taking extreme anti-Catholic, anti-French and "Rule Britannia" positions. (The equivalent of today's sucking-up to the Americans.) The annual Orange Parade was the biggest regular public event in Toronto until half way through the twentieth century and three of Canada's first five prime ministers were members of the Orange Order, including the first, John A. Macdonald.

Much to some people's surprise, the French-English rivalry started before hockey was even invented. It has been the tango of Canadian politics for over 200 years. In 1791, the province of Canada was split in two so that the Loyalists and other mostly British settlers could have English laws and institutions and be a majority in the new Upper Canada. The French-speaking majority in Lower Canada saw this as meaning that Britain conceded to them a distinct society, including their own legal system and Catholicism as the dominant religion. This was a big deal, because at the time Catholics could not legally hold public office in England. The creation of Upper Canada and selection of York on the north side of Lake Ontario as its capital a few years later, also laid the foundation for the race to be the biggest city in Canada contest between Toronto and Montréal, which right now Hogtown is leading.

Upper Canada was a baby when the War of 1812 once again threatened the existence of British North America. Fortunately for Canada, the First Nations were pissed off at the Americans for stealing their land and so helped fight the invading U.S. armies. They preferred the British, who sometimes kept their word, to the Americans who always lied, cheated and used military force to take what they wanted. And French Canada once again refused to heed the call of the Yankee traders. The lure of the republic could not overcome the linguistic, legal and religious accommodations previously made by the British. Working together, the Canadian militias, First Nations warriors and British army battled the Americans to a standoff. This was seen as pretty sweet. So sweet, in fact, the biggest candy and chocolate chain in Canada is named after a heroine of the war.

Over the next few decades, loyalty to Empire and attempts at replicating all that was British dominated the land, at least in upper class circles. London-appointed lieutenant-governors controlled political power. They favoured local "aristocracies" called the Chateau Clique in Lower Canada and the Family Compact in Upper Canada. While the colonial assemblies were far from democratic, they quickly became the focus of grievances. In Lower Canada, Scots, English and Irish colonists flooded in and while rural areas remained overwhelmingly French and Catholic, Montréal developed into a predominantly English-speaking city with a Scots-English ruling class. The government of Lower Canada supported the protectionist interests of that ruling class, but the assembly, with many members who came from French-speaking, rural areas, often fought for free trade policies that favoured farmers. In Upper Canada, there was also a growing split between the self-serving Family Compact and the farmers, shop owners and artisans who were flooding into the colony, often from the United States. In both colonies, distinctly Canadian revolutions broke out. In Lower Canada the overwhelming majority voted for democratic reform, but the Chateau Clique refused to give up its power and in 1837 the Patriotes took up arms. Before fighting even began their supposed leader, Louis Joseph Papineau, former speaker of the assembly, fled to the United States and the Patriotes were quickly defeated by British troops. The Upper Canada Rebellion, which began after reformers there heard about what was happening in Lower Canada, was led by William Lyon Mackenzie, the first mayor of Toronto and a newspaper publisher. The rebellion involved a few armed skirmishes, before Mackenzie also fled to the United States. Both groups of rebels later tried to organize invasions from the USA, but never managed to assemble more than a few easily defeated bands of guys with guns.

As a result of the rebellions, the British government sent over "Radical Jack" Lord Durham to come up with ways to solve the Canadian problem. His report essentially said "give the reformers what they want" but "let's screw the Frenchies" who started it all. Even though many of the Patriotes were, in fact, English, Scots and Irish. As a result, Upper and Lower Canada was made one colony, with the English-speaking minority getting the same number of seats in the new assembly as the French-speaking majority. As well, they made English the only official language in the assembly. It didn't take a steam-engine scientist to figure out what would happen next.

But, in what would become typical Canadian fashion, rather than another outbreak of violence, the new political system discovered creative compromise and accommodation. The story, according to the National Film Board, goes more or less like this: Most French Canadians and some English-speaking reformers (and the Family Compact in Upper Canada who lost power) were pretty pissed at the 1840 Act of Union that created the new colony of Canada. In the first election to the new assembly English-speaking thugs prevented supporters of a popular French-Canadian nationalist politician named Louis Hippolyte Lafontaine from voting, resulting in his defeat. Over in Toronto, Robert Baldwin, a believer in responsible government who had not supported the 1837 rebellion, was elected in two ridings (running in multiple ridings was okay in those days) and got the brilliant idea of offering Lafontaine the chance to run in a by-election in one of them. He did and won. Together, Baldwin and Lafontaine built a new Liberal party that united French and English speaking reformers. Within a decade they had won responsible government for the colony of Canada and overturned many of the anti-French aspects of the Act of Union. The key to Canadian political success had been discovered: To win, a political party needs to unite French and English in some common cause.

At Confederation in 1867, when the British North America Act created the new country, Canada had four provinces — Ontario, Québec, Nova Scotia and New Brunswick — but the political reality remained the same. Winning a federal election required a party that could bridge the divide between French and English speakers. This inevitably led to compromise and the equally old Canadian political tradition of things never being quite settled and people not being quite satisfied, which we've grown to kind of like.

From the beginning of Canada as a more or less independent country the government was faced with the commercial reality that our natural economic trading partner is the United States and the political reality that the country can survive only by distancing itself from the Manifest Destiny of the giant neighbour to the south. Our fathers of Confederation, including the first Canadian prime minister, John A. MacDonald, and his Québec lieutenant George Étienne Cartier, understood that the point of Canada as an independent country was to not be the United States. They wanted a British North America that stretched from the Atlantic to the Pacific and was a rival to our southern neighbour. The French-Canadian nationalist Cartier (he had to leave Canada for a year after the 1837 rebellion) and the Orange Order Conservative MacDonald each had their reasons for being anti-American and wanting to build Canada into an economic rival to the United States. For Cartier, an independent, strong Canada seemed a better bet to preserve French. For Macdonald and the Orange Order, the very essence of Canada was to not be the United States, but rather a part of the British Empire.

So, the point of Confederation in 1867 was to create an east-west economy from the Atlantic Ocean along the St. Lawrence River through the Great Lakes and then ultimately extend the new country to the Pacific Ocean by building a transcontinental railway. This plan required "acquiring" the northwestern part of the continent from the Hudson's Bay Company. At the time, the crazy idea that a company based in England could "own" millions of square kilometers inhabited by dozens of First Nations was considered perfectly reasonable. Among the first important pieces of legislation passed by the Canadian Parliament was the Rupert's Land Act of 1868, which transferred control of the Hudson's Bay Company land to the new Dominion government. Little or no consideration was given to the interests of the people who actually lived in the area sold.

Instead 300,000 pounds was paid to the Bay and the company "retained" the right to 20% of all the arable land. This failure to consider the people who lived on the land would result in two armed rebellions, which made Louis Riel among the best-known names in Canadian history.

From the moment these insurrections began, the country was divided over which side to support. In French Canada, Riel was a hero defending the rights of French Catholics, while in English Canada he was a dangerous, mentally unstable, traitor.

The First Riel Rebellion occurred soon after Confederation. The mostly French-speaking Metis (descendents of First Nations and Europeans), who had settled along the rivers near present-day Winnipeg, became alarmed that their interests were not represented in the handover of Rupert's Land to the new government of Canada. They formed a provisional government that militarily resisted the Canadian governor sent to run the territory. This English-speaking governor sent out surveyors to mark the land into one-mile squares, as in the United States. The Metis landholdings were in the French manner of long, narrow strips running back from river frontage. Eventually the provisional government negotiated the creation of a new province, where — on paper at least — the rights of both French and English would be respected. Louis Riel was celebrated, especially in French-speaking Canada, as the founder of Canada's fifth province, Manitoba, in 1870. Unfortunately, rather than being cheered in English-speaking Canada, he was charged with murder for his role in the provisional government's execution of a pro-Canada Orangeman named Thomas Scott. The Orange Order used the execution to stir up anti-French and anti-Catholic prejudice in Ontario. Despite Riel being elected three times to Parliament, the pressure for his arrest was so great that he had to flee Canada.

Fifteen years after the creation of Manitoba the continued poor treatment of the Metis by the Canadian government and the building of the Canadian Pacific Railway through First Nations' territory, resulted in the North-West Rebellion. Following the Red River Rebellion and an influx of settlers from Ontario, many of the Metis fled Manitoba and settled in the South Saskatchewan River valley. When, once again, Canadian government surveyors showed up to threaten their land holdings, in 1885 the Metis invited Riel back from the United States. They declared a provisional government, hoping to force the federal government to recognize a new province just like before. Upping the ante, this time the Metis tried to get the First Nations to join the rebellion, but most did not. After a Metis military force led by Gabriel Dumont defeated the North West Mounted Police and volunteers at the Battle of Duck Lake, the federal government sent 3,000 Canadian soldiers west. While the Metis and their First Nation allies defeated the army in a few battles, the superior force ultimately put down the rebellion. Riel and eight First Nations leaders were hanged. Dumont, who advocated guerilla warfare, not direct battle, which would have been more successful, escaped to the United States and became a marksman in the Wild West Show. A century later both rebels, Riel and Dumont, had been honoured with schools, colleges, and entire school districts bearing their names.

One of the key reasons for the defeat of the North-West Rebellion was the new Canadian Pacific Railway that enabled the government to send troops quickly. A few months after the fighting was over, the last spike was driven, finally connecting British Columbia with the rest of the country. The railway had taken so long to finish because a worldwide depression began in 1873. It wasn't until the Long Depression ended in the mid 1890s that the new east-west link finally started to pay dividends, as hundreds of thousands of settlers swarmed on to the flat lands of what would become Saskatchewan and Alberta in 1905. The period from 1896 to 1912 was the greatest boom in Canadian history. The National Policy, introduced by the Conservative Party in 1879 to favour Canadian industry through tariffs and other measures, enjoyed its greatest success in this period. Mills and manufacturing plants were built in Ontario and Québec to supply the western settlers with farm implements and other goods. B.C. lumber was shipped to build houses. Orchards in Nova Scotia, Ontario and B.C. boomed as they fed growing populations across the country. The port of Vancouver quickly grew into one of the largest on the Pacific coast of the Americas to ship goods to and from Asia. Winnipeg boomed as the warehousing hub of Manitoba and the new provinces of Saskatchewan and Alberta. Towns sprung up all across the prairies and some grew into sizeable cities, such as Regina, Saskatoon, Calgary and Edmonton.

But not everyone agreed with the National Policy. The Liberal Party wanted free trade with the United States, which they called Reciprocity. Elections in 1891 (won by the Conservatives) and 1896 (won by the Liberals) were largely fought on the issue of Reciprocity versus National Policy. In 1911 the Liberals signed a free trade deal with the United States and promptly lost the election that year. The winning Conservative slogan was "No truck or trade with the Yankees" and it was quickly back to the National Policy.

The First World War gave another major boost to Canadian industry, but also killed tens of thousands of young men who marched off to bolster Britain's ranks. As part of the Empire, Canada automatically joined Great Britain when it declared war against Germany in 1914. At first Canadian troops fought under British officers but later thousands were slaughtered under the command of their fellow countrymen. This has been described as the real birth of Canada by some of our more militaristically inclined, but it could be equally argued that the First World War was the birth of a debate that divides the country to this day. What should Canada's military policy be? Should we automatically join in when our allies engage in war or should we take a more neutral policy? Should Canada have an independent foreign policy? If so, what should it be?

Many Canadians opposed the First World War. Socialists, anarchists and union members, especially in western Canada, were philosophically opposed to capitalist wars. Various immigrant groups such as Dukobors and Mennonites were pacifists. And French-speaking Canadians were widely hostile to the war, partly because the army discriminated against them. As well, a law was passed in Ontario in 1912 forbidding the use of French in schools, so it seemed to Québecers that fighting a war in Europe under the banner of King and Country, with English officers commanding them, didn't make much sense. When the Conservative prime minister pushed through the Military Services Act to force men to fight, the result was the Conscription Crisis of 1917. Riots occurred in Québec and across the country tens of thousands of men refused to report for war. The most famous individual case was that of Ginger Goodwin, a union organizer in British Columbia, who was shot dead, sparking the first general strike in Canadian history in 1918 in Vancouver. Another result of the Conscription Crisis was that the Conservative Party was pretty much shut out of winning seats in Québec for the next 40 years.

Most of Canada had a booming economy in the 1920s, but the Great Depression of the 1930s hit the country, especially the western provinces, hard. In parts of Saskatchewan and Alberta a drought decimated farmers. Hundreds of thousands of workers lost their jobs and young people who would normally have entered the labour force were instead forced to "ride the rails" — hitching free rides on freight trains that moved across the country in a hopeless search for work. The Conservative government responded by creating relief camps — some called them forced labour centres — where thousands of young men built roads, parks, airports and other public projects for extremely low wages and lived in very poor conditions under military-type control. The camps turned out to be perfect recruiting centres for the Communist Party and the new Cooperative Commonwealth Federation (CCF) a social democratic party created in 1932.

Thanks to the depression, Conservative Prime Minister R.B. Bennett, who was elected in 1930, became one of the most disliked politicians in Canadian history. Not until 1935, did his government respond to the economic crisis with an activist approach, finally mimicking the New Deal of U.S. President Franklin Delano Roosevelt. It was too little, too late, and the Conservatives were driven from office for over twenty years.

An important long-term change in Canadian politics that occurred in this period was the conversion of the Liberals from the party of free trade (especially attractive to some farming communities) and French rights to the party of progressive social change. Some argue the Liberals under William Lyon Mackenzie King, the country's longest-serving prime minister, were forced to the political left by the growing strength of the CCF. Another reading of history is that King's goal was to move the country away from Great Britain and towards the United States. While he stole enough of the CCF platform to stunt the growth of the socialist party, he was simply following in the Liberal pro-American tradition (he was personally close to important U.S. capitalists, having worked for the Rockefellers earlier in his career). His government certainly passed no laws more radical than those of the Democratic Party under FDR.

The Second World War was very good for the Canadian economy as the country helped supply Britain and the allies with food, manufactured goods and raw materials. The war and the period immediately afterwards also saw the growth of industrial unions, a rise in popularity of Canada's socialist party, the CCF, and the creation of social programs such as pensions, workers compensation and unemployment insurance. The Liberal Party continued its successful two-pronged "progressive" approach to governing. On the one hand, it was an activist government that introduced new social programs. On the other, it began re-orienting Canada's foreign and economic policy away from the British and towards the expanding USA empire. The pro-U.S. shift was seen as progressive because it was part of a process of dismantling the British Empire. The Liberals built a coalition of its old pro-U.S. (pro-free-trade) base that included many Canadian business interests, French-speaking Canada and left-liberal voters who thought it safer to vote for a mainstream party that would gradually introduce some socialist measures rather than trust the more radical CCF.

This was a successful governing formula for over 40 years with the Liberals in power from 1935 to 1984, except for the Diefenbaker years from 1957-1963 and nine months of 1979-80. Interestingly, the sole successful Conservative Party leader during this five-decade long period was John Diefenbaker, a populist, somewhat "anti-American" (but mostly pro-British, in the Conservative Party tradition) politician who managed to win one majority government with the support of a right-wing, nationalist Québec government in the 1958 election. He was also seen as progressive in many important ways. He introduced Canada's first bill of rights, criticized apartheid South Africa, extended voting rights to "status Indians" and stopped nuclear warheads from being deployed on U.S. missiles located in Canada. But, for most of his time in power the economy did relatively poorly and his modest "anti-Americanism" proved too much for important business interests. So, he was toppled in an internal party coup after losing two elections to the long-time pro-American foreign affairs bureaucrat and former ambassador to the U.S., Lester Pearson.

Pearson, who won the Nobel Peace Prize for his role in the 1957 Suez Crisis and is credited by some with the concept of peacekeeping missions, was prime minister in two minority governments that probably passed more progressive legislation than any other in Canadian history. Historians will argue endlessly whether this was because of his convictions or political reality. Pearson never managed to win a majority, so his Liberals governed with the support of the New Democratic Party, which was created in 1961 by the CCF and most of Canada's largest unions. To get the support of this new socialist party his governments passed laws mandating a 40-hour work week, mandatory two weeks vacation, an increased minimum wage, created the Canada Pension Plan, created a national universal healthcare plan, instituted a point system for immigrants (to replace the previous racist system), began the process of creating official bilingualism and equal rights for women, and introduced Canada's new flag. To this day, Pearson is hated by fanatic pro-British types for choosing the Maple Leaf. Pearson's governments also refused to formally send troops to fight in the Vietnam War, although behind the scenes Canada was very much involved in supporting the USA. And one of Pearson's first acts as prime minister was to accept U.S. nuclear missiles on Canadian soil.

The next Liberal prime minister, Pierre Trudeau, is, to this day, the best-known politician that Canada ever produced. Flamboyant and arrogant, Trudeau was part of a generation in Québec that laid the intellectual foundations for what came to be known as the Quiet Revolution. This was the period in the 1960s when Québecers went rapidly from being the most religious and most conservative in Canada to the least religious and most socially progressive people, many of whom no longer wanted to be part of Canada. Trudeau was representative of the trajectory of the Quiet Revolution and it went something like this: The French-speaking elite was educated in Jesuit schools where corporatist, pro-fascist ideas were popular in the late 1930s. The Second World War, travel and exposure to the intellectual ferment of the post-war period transformed the well-educated elite into a conduit exposing the entire Québec society to ideas of class, nationalism, counterculture and secularism. The explanation for the speed of the Quiet Revolution was the relatively small size and interconnected, almost familial, nature of Québec society, so the route from elite to mass consumption was short. La Belle Province underwent a greater transformation in the 1960s than any other place in North America, even more than hippie havens of free love like San Francisco or Vancouver. Trudeau is best remembered as an icon of the contradictions of that process. He is regarded as a progressive liberal and a Canadian nationalist by those who cite his remark about keeping the state out of our bedrooms during the debate about legalizing homosexuality, or for his government's willingness to allow U.S. draft dodgers into the country and for his 1982 Constitution. But he is equally seen, especially in his hometown, as an archenemy of Québec nationalism, willing to suspend civil liberties and send the army into the streets to crush dissent. Trudeau's invocation of the War Measures Act in 1970 after the tiny FLQ (Front de Liberation du Québec) kidnapped a British diplomat and then a provincial cabinet minister, was popular across Canada, but a huge affront to the growing nationalist movement of Québec.

In fact, two "progressive" nationalisms arose during the Quiet Revolution — Québec and Canadian — and they competed against each other for support. Both also fought a rearguard battle with the forces of an old order. Understanding those two nationalisms and the old orders each faced is the key to making sense of the past four decades of Canadian political history.

To quickly sum up the Québec nationalist narrative: The French-speaking people of Canada were colonized and, like oppressed nations around the world, deserve independence and their own national government. That national aspiration finds its realistic territorial expression in Québec, therefore the province should become a separate country. And the Canadian nationalist narrative: The various peoples that comprise Canada have suffered under governments and economic systems that were never truly Canadian, but rather, served the interests of first Britain and then the USA. The goal is to build a government and economy that serves Canadian interests. The French-speaking people of Canada are one of our founding nations and essential to what makes us distinct.

Québec nationalists tend to believe theirs is the only real nation in Canada and view Canadian nationalism as, at best, unrealistic or, at worst, just another trap to keep Québec oppressed. Canadian nationalists tend to see Québec nationalism as, at best, settling for too little, or, at worst, narrow, inward looking and potentially fascist. Both sides do, in fact, have sound reasons to believe the worst of the other. The federal government has turned to Canadian nationalism as a way of blunting Québec's national aspirations. In fact, since Pearson and especially Trudeau's time most federal legislation has been shaped by considerations of managing the "threat" from Québec nationalism. Medicare, other social programs and expansions of the federal government's role in the economy were designed, in part, to prove that Ottawa was relevant to Québec. And Canadian nationalists can point to periods when right-wing reactionaries who called for some form of "ethnic" purity dominated Québec nationalism.

While the two nationalisms fought each other, both had to contend with "old orders" that opposed progress. In the case of Québec, the new "progressive" nationalism had to create a coalition with the old "reactionary" nationalism in order to win elections, while at the same time fighting off defenders of the old (pro-Empire, pro-Canada) status quo and the new Canadian nationalism. In English Canada the new nationalists had to contend with the old pro-U.S. free trade forces and remnants of the Orange Order-United Empire Loyalist crowd. The history of Canada from the 1970s through today can be seen as a series of interactions among these forces.

While the Liberals under Pearson and Trudeau were forced to move to the left and promote Canadian nationalism as an alternative to Québec nationalism, the Conservative Party of the 1980s and early 90s under Brian Mulroney found a winning strategy by creating a coalition of Québec nationalists, old-time Tories and pro-U.S. free traders in business and other communities. The result was the North American Free Trade Agreement (NAFTA) and the empowering of pro-USA sentiments and U.S.-like politics. Mulroney's coalition was not, however, stable. A right wing, evangelical, populist-sounding, pro-U.S., anti-Québec rump formed, mostly in western Canada and split away to create the Reform Party. The splitting of the right-of-centre vote gave successive majority governments to the Liberals who governed through the 1990s from the right on the economic side and from the liberal-left on the social side. Unable to break through nationally as the Reform Party the right created the Alliance Party and then took over the Progressive Conservatives and re-branded it the Conservative Party. In 2006 they won an election and formed a minority government. They were reelected in 2008, once again as a minority.

The differences over the past few decades between the

Liberals and Conservatives were sometimes substantial on social issues, but on economic policy they followed the same playbook. Both abandoned any semblance of a national policy and instead pursued integration of the North American economy within an overall strategy of de-industrialization and expansion of the financial sector. While this apparently made sense to the wealthiest Canadians, the result for the country was a Canada in which the steel industry, the biggest mining companies, the auto industry, the oil sector and even much of the forestry sector became foreign-owned. Liberal and Conservative policies led to a situation where there was not much of a Canadian economy left to protect or direct. Instead, most economic power was handed over to the boardrooms of multinational companies.

And that's about it. If you remember everything in this chapter you'll know more about our history than the average Canadian.

Except, I did leave out one important theme. It's important enough that it gets a chapter all to itself.

You know who really gets me going? Right-wingers who pretend to be the worker's friend. There's got to be some sort of school somewhere supplying a steady stream of radio talk show hosts, newspaper columnists, TV celebrity idiots, preachers and politicians who would have you believe the world is a better place when there's war going on, that hating someone for who they love makes sense, that whether you got balls or a vagina should limit your role in the world, that foreigners are, at a minimum, not to be trusted and often bombed, that some left-wing elite runs the media when anyone with half a brain knows rich people own it, control it and hire the dumb-ass right-wingers who then claim a left-wing elite is out to fool you.

# CHAPTER 4

# Immigrants R Us

Our geography, our form of government, our history and the lies we tell about ourselves have all had a part in creating who we are today. But there is another key ingredient in the recipe for understanding Canada: immigration.

About 14.5 million people immigrated to this country between 1901 and 2006 and another quarter-million or so per year since. Of course this has had a profound effect on who we are and who we are becoming.

Relative to the population of the country (31.6 million in 2006), the 1.2 million immigrants arriving in the five years from 2001 to 2006 meant Canada had the highest legal migration rate in the world. According to the OECD, Canada had a net 6.5 migrants per 1,000-population between 2000-2004. (Australia was second, accepting 6.2 migrants per 1,000-population during the same period.) About 70% of Canada's five-year population growth rate of 5.4% (1.6 million more people) from 2001-2006 came from immigration.

At the time of the 2006 census, 19.8% of Canada's population were born outside the country, the second highest rate of foreign born in the world after Australia's 22.2%. In contrast, the U.S. rate was 12.5%.

Canada attracts new citizens from every ethnic group and all corners of the world. Of the 1.2 million immigrants who arrived between 2001 and 2006, 58% came from Asia, including the Middle East; 16% from Europe; 11% from the Caribbean, Central and South America; 10.5% from Africa; and 3.5% from the United States. Compare that to a planet where about 61% of the population is Asian, 12% is European, 13% African, 9% from South America and the Caribbean, and 5% North American.

Of course, Canada's immigration policy was not always so liberal. While the country has almost always actively recruited immigrants, much of the time it has also actively discouraged people from most of the world. In fact, racist and discriminatory best describe Canada's official policy from the first immigration act in 1869 to 1967.

Legislation passed in 1885, 1900 and 1903 placed restrictions on and imposed a "head tax" on Chinese immigrants. In 1923 virtually all immigrants from Asia were excluded. A 1906 act was influenced by the supposedly scientific eugenics theories popular at the time and people judged "defective" such as prostitutes, the mentally ill, and epileptics (this didn't, of course, apply to the British "remittance men" who could be all three, but came from the "better" classes) were banned. A 1910 act gave the cabinet power to regulate immigration and in 1919 Doukhabours, Hutterites and Mennonites were prohibited from entering Canada because they were pacifist religions. (If you had to choose, would you pick members of pacifist or war-like religions? I guess you had to have been there.) In 1952, new legislation gave the cabinet authority to deny entry based on "nationality, customs, or unsuitability to the Canadian climate or culture" — code for discrimination on the basis of crackpot racial theories. In 1956 regulations were changed to give "favoured" nation status to Britain, the USA and some Commonwealth countries. Finally, in 1967, the new immigration act removed all racial discrimination from legislation, but it wasn't until 1978 that Canada's official policy became one of multicultural immigration.

Currently, to become an immigrant to Canada you must qualify for one of five basic categories:

**Skilled workers or professional.** It's all about accumulating points through a combination of education, experience and language skills.

**Investors, entrepreneurs and self-employed.** Money talks; an absence of it means you head to the back of the line.

**Family sponsorship.** Once one member of your family becomes a citizen or a permanent resident you too can qualify.

**A provincial nominee.** Most provinces have deals to get you in quicker if some company wants your trade or profession. Québec is big in this area to ensure immigrants fit into a French-speaking society.

**A refugee.** You can apply as a refugee from outside Canada or inside. Just make sure not to enter the country from the U.S. or you could be screwed, because you have to apply for refugee status there. Becoming a refugee is a long, bureaucratically complicated process but Canada does provide a new home for thousands of at risk people every year.

While polls consistently find that the majority (typically 65-75%) of us believes the country benefits from its new citizens and thinks the current level of immigration is about right, they also reveal a substantial minority who don't like newcomers. Perhaps this is inevitable because a certain proportion of every population is scared of or doesn't like outsiders. Personal experience suggests a tiny (one in a hundred or so) hardcore of Canadians passionately oppose immigration. Most are racists, but some are simply cranky xenophobes. But there is a much larger minority (perhaps 20-25% of the population) who are quietly negative about immigrants in general and non-English-speaking ones in particular. Some political parties tap into this sentiment, but being too overtly anti-immigrant has become a vote killer in Canada. There are simply too many immigrants, their children who are now citizens, and too many other Canadians who believe in immigration.

Our governments and other institutions have been successful at convincing the majority of Canadians that "multiculturalism" makes sense for this country. Of course, like most things, you have to live here awhile to figure what the Beliveau (pardon my French) multiculturalism really means. And some Canadians, especially of the dull, rightwing sort, have never figured it out because subtlety and nuance are involved. We call the policy multiculturalism and, on the surface, this means that immigrants are encouraged to hold onto their various ethnic backgrounds and we celebrate our differences. We even claim Canada is a "mosaic" as opposed to the American "melting pot" but the opposite is actually true. Wise Canadians discovered decades ago that the very best way to absorb millions of newcomers from all around the world, while avoiding ghettos, is to proclaim that we value all cultures equally. We tell immigrants that we respect their ways of doing things, their religions; we add that Canada is a cultural mosaic and we celebrate our differences.

In return for this generosity of spirit, Canadian immigrants assimilate better than those of any other country in the world. In fact, based on actual results, Canadian multiculturalism is much better than the so-called American melting pot at producing a curry where all the spices blend together to create a harmonious new flavour. It's like subtle Canadian humour, where words often mean the opposite of what the dictionary tells us. Canadian multiculturalism produces a melting pot, while the American so-called melting pot produces ghettos that last for generations.

Of course the key is that most Canadians never had a strong sense of who we are, so we couldn't be like the Americans, or French, or German, or Dutch or English who long ago defined their stereotypes and could demand that immigrants fit into that idealized national standard. The real meaning of multiculturalism is that anyone who chooses to belong can be Canadian but leaves vague exactly what that means. It allows millions of immigrants to be "hyphenated Canadians" and in fact celebrates the concept of a dual, even multiple, identity.

Multiculturalism has made sense to most Canadians because it, in fact, describes what has been happening. Our definition of Canadian for the past four decades has been rather simple: We are those people who are engaged in the process of becoming Canadian. The brilliance of this definition is that it defines people who don't like newcomers as un-Canadian. And that has gone a long way in maintaining our civility towards newcomers, unlike many other parts of the world where immigrants are viewed as outsiders until they "fit in" with the established culture, or remain outsiders forever because they are of the wrong ethnic or religious background.

Canada has been more successful at integrating newcomers into the mainstream than anywhere else in the world. But the process is dynamic and always fragile. While it is relatively easy to keep xenophobia in check while the economy is booming, what happens in a recession or depression?

The good news for supporters of immigration is that recent surveys show that Canadians under 40 are very comfortable with multiculturalism and tend to be strong internationalists. This is, of course, the reality that our younger generations know. Multiculturalism describes their experience. A high percentage of people under the age of 40 in Canada have grown up with neighbours, schoolmates, teammates, workmates and friends who are immigrants, or the children of immigrants, from China, India, Somalia, Chile, Nigeria, Pakistan, Eritrea, El Salvador, Uganda, Vietnam, Palestine, Russia, Korea, South Africa, Mexico or a hundred other countries. Our young people especially have learned to get along and work together. Their reality is multicultural and internationalist and they seem to like it.

But recent immigrants to Canada have not spread out evenly across the country. For the past two decades over 80% of them headed to Canada's biggest cities. These are the places becoming more and more like the world as a whole.

To a large extent, our most recent Canadian culture has been developing in the neighbourhoods, schools, workplaces, parks, stores, community centres, churches and sports arenas of Toronto, Vancouver and Montréal. Of course, some people spend only a few years in these places before moving on to another part of Canada (about 73% of immigrants who arrived in the 1990s remained in the three cities in 2001), but the importance of these three cities, even for immigrants who subsequently move on, is critical. Four out of five immigrants first learn what it means to "be Canadian" in Toronto, Vancouver or Montréal. And, in 2006, over 40% of all Canadians, 13.9 million people, were living in the Montréal census metropolitan area, the Vancouver census metropolitan area, and the Greater Golden Horseshoe (centered on Toronto) in southern Ontario.

Because an immigrant never really moves to a country, but rather to a neighbourhood in a town, city or rural area, the creation of the "new Canadian" is occurring in those places. Ultimately, culture is local.

Toronto, Vancouver and Montréal are and will likely continue to be at the forefront of where our new Canadian culture is built. So, to understand Canada, it is important to take a look at what is happening on the street corner, TTC, SkyTrain and Metro of these three cities.

## Toronto

They once called this place Hogtown because of the slaughterhouses, but now people think the nickname refers to how Toronto has eaten up so much of the land around it to become, by far, the biggest urban area in Canada. The municipality of Toronto had 2.5 million people in 2006, in a metropolitan area of 5.1 million, surrounded by a place Statistics Canada calls the Greater Golden Horseshoe, with 8.1 million people, that stretches from Port Hope to Kitchener-Waterloo and from Barrie down to Niagara Falls. It hogs one quarter of the people and an even bigger chunk of the nation's political and economic power. Half of Canada's manufacturing economy is located here, plus it is the headquarters for all of the country's big banks and most major corporations.

But being big isn't enough, because there's always Biggar (a small town in Saskatchewan) and some people in Toronto are constantly judging the place, from opera halls to neighbourhoods, to baseball stadiums, to tall buildings, against the Big Apple. Forgive them because theirs was a newer York (the original name for Toronto) than New York when the Americans in the War of 1812 burned the town to the ground and they've been trying to catch up ever since.

This new bigger Toronto, or Greater Golden Horseshoe, is where over half of all immigrants over the past two decades first tried on their new parkas and learned hockey etiquette. The good news is that the city is the real united nations. You can arrive here from any part of the globe and there's an excellent chance of finding a cousin, not more than a couple times removed. The bad news is that half of all our Canadian newcomers become Maple Leaf fans. The compromise is: Toronto gets the head offices and economic growth, but in return must live with the Maple Leafs. A fundamental Toronto experience is getting into a cab in October and having the driver, who arrived two years earlier from the Punjab, tell you how the Leafs are going to win the Stanley Cup, for certain, yes they will, this season. Why, the team's fourth line could be the first line on many NHL squads! While one can feel pity, it is strangely gratifying to realize how Torontonians themselves pay the biggest price for living in the centre of the Canadian media universe. They really do believe, at least until January, or in a good year, April. Then the city becomes next year country, like the two coasts after poor fishing seasons or the prairies after bad harvests. Perhaps the Maple Leafs are part of a grand Canadian plan to teach our many Toronto newcomers the very Canadian virtue of remaining optimistic in the face of an ugly reality.

What happens when people from all over the world come together to live in one place? A team of Sri Lankans works in the kitchen to make Japanese-French fusion cuisine for a private party celebrating the engagement of a second generation Jamaican-Canadian physician to a Hong Kong-based stockbroker who holds dual Canadian and Chinese citizenship. Friends and family from all over Toronto have about the same ethnic makeup as a session of the General Assembly.

Just over 40% of all immigrants who came to Canada from 2001 to 2006 lived in the census metropolitan area (CMA) of Toronto in 2006.

### Toronto's ethnic origin Top 20
(includes multiple responses)

| | |
|---|---|
| Total population | 5,113,149 |
| English | 804,100 |
| Canadian | 651,635 |
| Scottish | 561,050 |
| Chinese | 537,060 |
| Irish | 531,865 |
| East Indian | 484,655 |
| Italian | 466,155 |
| German | 259,015 |
| French | 241,395 |
| Polish | 207,495 |
| Portuguese | 188,110 |
| Filipino | 181,330 |
| Jamaican | 160,205 |
| Jewish | 141,685 |
| Ukrainian | 122,510 |
| Russian | 102,815 |
| Spanish | 97,255 |
| Dutch | 95,560 |
| Greek | 90,585 |
| Sri Lankan | 80,610 |

Residents of CMA Toronto reported over 200 ethnic origins, the top 94 of which included at least 5,000 people in each.

The old Toronto of the Orange Order parade has been replaced by a new planetary metropolis in which over one quarter of the population speaks a language other than English (or French) at home and self-identification with

British Isles ancestry is barely over one-quarter (26.3%) of the population. Of the 5,072,070 residents in CMA Toronto in 2006, 2,174,065 identified themselves as members of a visible minority. (Some people argue this is a racist term. At a minimum it veers into an absurd realm when "visible minority" actually is a majority. But, since it is the term used in census data, it will be used here.) They comprised 42.9% of Toronto's total population, up from 36.8% in 2001, 31.6% in 1996 and 25.8% in 1991. About 29% of residents in CMA Toronto identified themselves as Asian in 2006, up from 24% in 2001, 20% in 1996 and 16% in 1991.

The largest visible minority group, South Asian, was also the fastest growing. From 1991 to 2001 to 2006, they went from 235,500 to 473,800 to 684,070 and represented 13.5% of Toronto's population in 2006, up from 10% in 2001 and 6% in 1991. Just over 72% of South Asians in Toronto in 2006 were born outside of Canada.

A total of 486,330 people in CMA Toronto identified themselves as Chinese in 2006, up from 409,500 in 2001 and 242,300 a decade earlier, accounting for 9.6% of its total population, up from 9% in 2001 and 6% in 1991. Just less than 75% of Chinese in Toronto were foreign-born in 2006.

Toronto had 352,220 people who identified themselves as Black, up from 241,000 in 1991. They accounted for 6.9% of Toronto's population, compared to 7% in 2001 and 6% in 1991. Just over 55% of Toronto's Black population in 2006 was foreign-born.

Toronto also had 171,985 Filipinos (over 73% foreign-born), accounting for 3.4% of its population, up from nearly

3% in 2001 and 2% in 1991. Other sizeable visible minority groups included Latin Americans (99,290), West Asians (75,500), Southeast Asians (70,200), Koreans (55,300), Arabs (53,400) and Japanese (19,000). All those communities grew significantly since 1991. About 11% of immigrants who moved to Toronto in the 1990s came from the People's Republic of China, 10% from India, and 7% each from the Philippines and Hong Kong. Other top countries of origin included Sri Lanka, Pakistan, Jamaica, Iran, Poland and Guyana. About 82% of all immigrants who came to Toronto from 2001-2006 were visible minorities compared to 79% during the 1990s and 73% in the 1980s.

Of course, both visible minorities and immigrants in general are not spread evenly throughout the census metropolitan area. Almost two-thirds (65.4%) of the population of Markham, a northern suburb, was comprised of visible minorities in 2006 up from 56% in 2001 and 46% in 1996. Over half (52.4%) of Markham's visible "minority" was Chinese and over one-quarter (26.4%) was South Asian.

Visible minorities comprised 46.9% of the population of the city of Toronto, 45.7% in Richmond Hill (another northern suburb), 49.0% in Mississauga (a huge municipality to the west of the city) and 57.0% in the northwestern suburb of Brampton.

The multi-ethnic communities are now spreading past the confines of Toronto's census metropolitan area to towns and cities throughout the Golden Horseshoe and even beyond. For example, nearly one-quarter of the population in the census metropolitan area of Hamilton, to the south of Toronto at the head of Lake Ontario, in 2006, was foreign born, the third highest proportion in Canada after Vancouver and Toronto. Of the 166,630 residents in Hamilton who were born outside Canada, 20,785 (12.5%) were immigrants between 2001 and 2006. About 42% of these more recent newcomers came from Asia. But Europe was also a strong source of immigration. In 2006, Hamilton was home to 84,290 people who described themselves as members of a visible minority. This was 12.3% of the population, up from 10% in 2001 and 7% in 1991. While the visible minority communities have been growing, about half of Hamilton residents still have origins in the British Isles.

North of Hamilton, at the western edge of the Golden Horseshoe, 23.1% of the population (446,495) of the census metropolitan area of Kitchener (including Cambridge and Waterloo) was born outside Canada. Over half of the most recent (2003-2006) immigrants living in Kitchener in 2006 came from Asia. A total of 61,450 Kitchener residents belonged to a visible minority group, which was 13.8% of the population in 2006, up from 11% in 2001, and 8% in 1991. The two largest visible minority groups were South Asians, who made up 3.6% of Kitchener's total population, and Blacks, representing 2.1%. In addition, Chinese made up 2.0% of the population and Latin Americans 1.5%.

What do Toronto and the Golden Horseshoe tell us about Canadians? First, and most important, that people from all over the world have come together in relative harmony and are living a culture that is recognizably Canadian, but something more.

At an intramural soccer game on a downtown University of Toronto pitch a visitor from Pittsburgh might think he is watching squads from rival international students clubs, but every player was born in the Golden Horseshoe. At the nearby arena where women's varsity teams from the U of T and York are playing each other for the right to represent Ontario in the national hockey championship, the players and the fans have connections to over 100 countries, speak dozens of languages and come from every major religious tradition on the planet.

In 1950, pizza was an exotic dish in Toronto, Italians were widely considered an inferior race, Jews were barred from the best golf clubs, Chinese people were only recently allowed to vote and the Orange Parade drew larger crowds than the Eaton's Christmas Parade. As the first decade of the new millennium came to a close, who believes Italians are a "race" or that such a thing even exists? The Orange Order is mostly a historical curiosity and the faces lining the route of the mid-November 2009 Santa Claus parade were as often Chinese, like the Member of Parliament for the area of the parade route, or south Asian, as European.

Toronto is doing better than simply coping with its diversity. It is proud of it. Multiculturalism has become an economic selling point. Are there problems? Of course, this is, after all, the home of the Maple Leafs. But the biggest concerns are sprawl, housing and transportation, not how people from diverse backgrounds get along.

## Vancouver

The thing to understand about Vancouver is that people who live there generally think it is the best place in the world. And they expect newcomers to agree, despite the rain. This is not the Toronto "look we're world class too, like New York" kind of attitude that in fact proves an inferiority complex. Vancouverites believe, feel, know their hometown is as good as it gets because, well, it is — as a sunny day walk around the Stanley Park seawall, or a couple of hours on a sailboard in English Bay, or an afternoon's skiing on Grouse Mountain with the towers of downtown beneath you, reveals. Much more than a typical hometown boosterism, residents love the geographic setting — North Shore mountains plunging into the Pacific Ocean with rich delta soils stretching 100 kilometres up the flat Fraser Valley — the lush, mild climate — never too hot, never too cold, the only part of Canada where a winter might pass without snow, except up in the nearby mountains where you can ski for five months of the year — and tolerance of all kinds of diversity. All mainstream political parties participate in the Gay Pride parade and compete for candidates from every ethnic group.

Yet, from taking First Nations land, to a "head tax" on Chinese immigrants, to turning away British subjects from India on the ship Komagata Maru in 1912, to pre-First World War anti-Asian riots, to the legalized theft of Japanese-Canadian property during the Second World War, to limits on admission of Asians at the University of British Columbia until the 1960s and much more, Vancouver has a long history of racism and of fighting against it. Generally considered the most left-wing city in Canada, it has also been home to some of the most right wing, racist political movements in the country, such as the Ku Klux Klan in the 1930s.

While Toronto was transformed after the Second World War from a White Anglo-Saxon Protestant bastion, content to be a big dot on the biggest "pink part" of the globe, to a world metropolis, Vancouver became the most Asian city in North America. Perched on the Pacific Ocean, it always had strong Asian influences throughout its 150-year (non First Nations) history, but until recently this fact made many people in Vancouver uncomfortable. To be blunt, the city was a racist place. For example, land title covenants for Shaughnessy (a wealthy city neighbourhood) and the British Properties (an exclusive part of West Vancouver) disallowed Asian buyers until the 1960s. While eastside, working class parts of the city were always ethnically diverse, it was not until the 1980s' influx of billions of dollars worth of Hong Kong and Taiwan capital fleeing the possibility of confiscation by the Chinese government that the wealthier westside also began to take on a more Asian character.

Today, the census metropolitan area of Vancouver has the second highest proportion of visible minorities of any city in Canada and is one of the most diverse places in the world. Of CMA Vancouver's 2.1 million people, 875,300, or 41.7%, identified themselves as a member of a visible minority in 2006. That was up from 37% in 2001, 31% in 1996 and 24% in 1991. The Chinese population was 18.7% of the CMA Vancouver total, the highest proportion in Canada.

The Chinese population grew by 11.3% from 2001 to 2006, compared with an overall population gain of 6.6%, but the rate of growth of the Chinese population slowed, compared with the previous decade. South Asians were the second largest visible minority group, at 9.9% of the population, up from 8.4% in 2001. The percentage of people residing in Vancouver in 2006 who were born outside of Canada was 39.6%.

### Vancouver's ethnic origin Top 20

| | |
|---|---|
| Total population | 2,116,581 |
| English | 484,340 |
| Chinese | 402,000 |
| Scottish | 337,225 |
| Canadian | 278,350 |
| Irish | 251,695 |
| German | 203,720 |
| East Indian | 181,895 |
| French | 137,270 |
| Filipino | 83,765 |
| Ukrainian | 81,725 |
| Italian | 76,345 |
| Dutch | 71,715 |
| Polish | 60,715 |
| Russian | 47,940 |
| Norwegian | 46,260 |
| Korean | 46,035 |
| N. Amer. Indian | 43,190 |
| Welsh | 41,805 |
| Swedish | 39,920 |
| Spanish | 36,000 |

Interestingly, while Vancouver is the most Asian city in Canada, it still retains strong ties to the British Isles. Just over one third of the population reported at least one ancestor from the British Isles.

Just as in Toronto, the percentage of visible minority populations varies greatly by municipality. In the suburb just south of the city, Richmond, 65.1% of the population belonged to a visible minority group in 2006 up from 59% in 2001. This was the second highest in the country after 65.4% in Markham, Ontario. In the central suburb of Burnaby, 55.4% of the population belonged to a visible minority, while in the City of Vancouver it was 51.0%. In the suburb of Surrey it was 46.1%, in the eastern suburb of Coquitlam 38.6% and in New Westminster 29.6%.

Just as ethnic diversity has expanded out from Toronto into Ontario's Greater Golden Horseshoe, so too has it in the Lower Mainland of B.C. At 22.8% (up from 18% in 2001), the census metropolitan area of Abbotsford, which is in the Fraser Valley east of Vancouver, had the third highest proportion of visible minorities among major urban areas in Canada, after Vancouver and Toronto.

Like Toronto, the pace of change in Vancouver has been stunning over the past three decades. The population has more than doubled and most of the newcomers have come from Asia. But tens of thousands have also come from South America, Africa and Eastern Europe. Vancouver has the highest rate of intermarriage between religious and ethnic groups of any city in Canada. In 2006, 8.5% of all marriages in CMA Vancouver were between a visible minority person and someone who was from another visible minority or who was not from a visible minority. Toronto had the next highest proportion of mixed unions at 7.1%.

Like Toronto, Vancouver revels in its diversity. The city has tremendous social problems, especially homelessness and drug addiction, even though it regularly wins one of the top spots in best-places-to-live-in-the-world rankings. But diversity of all forms is widely held to be a strength, not a weakness. Even the gangs, as they fight to control the drug trade, are often ethnically diverse.

## Montréal

People are not unfriendly in downtown Montréal; they're just waiting for you to say something to know whether you speak English or French. In fact, not talking to strangers is their way of being polite. They don't want to offend you by starting a conversation in the wrong language. Montréal is a historically, politically and linguistically complicated city, which has had a profound effect on immigrants and immigration. The ethnic make-up of the city is much different from Toronto and Vancouver. One important Canadian irony is illustrated below. Despite being the largest city in the "separatist" province of Québec, the most common choice of describing one's ethnic origin is Canadian.

**Montréal's Top-20 ethnic groups**

| | |
|---|---|
| Total population | 3,635,571 |
| Canadian | 1,670,655 |
| French | 936,990 |
| Italian | 260,345 |

| | |
|---|---|
| Irish | 216,410 |
| English | 148,095 |
| Scottish | 119,365 |
| Haitian | 85,785 |
| Chinese | 82,665 |
| German | 78,315 |
| N. Amer. Indian | 74,565 |
| Québécois | 72,445 |
| Jewish | 68,485 |
| Greek | 61,770 |
| Spanish | 56,770 |
| Lebanese | 53,455 |
| Polish | 51,920 |
| Portuguese | 46,535 |
| East Indian | 39,305 |
| Romanian | 36,275 |
| Russian | 35,800 |

While Montréal was home to the third largest absolute number of visible minorities among the 27 census metropolitan areas in 2006 they accounted for only 16.5% of Montréal's population of 3,588,520, up from 13.5% in 2001 and 12.2% in 1996. In 2006, the national average was 16.2%. The composition of Montréal's visible minority population differed substantially from Toronto and Vancouver. Blacks (the biggest group from Haiti) represented almost 30% of all visible minorities, while Arabs represented almost 17%. (Counting Arabs as a visible minority, while Israelis and Iranians are not, is another of the absurdities of this term.)

There were 740,355 persons born outside Canada living in Montréal in 2006, representing 20.6% of the population, up from 18% in 2001 and 1996, and 16% in 1991. As in Toronto and Vancouver the percentage of visible minorities varied substantially by CMA municipality. Over one-third (34.4%) of Brossard's population belonged to a visible minority. It was followed by Dollard-des-Ormeaux (30.9%), the City of Montréal (26.0%), Mont-Royal (19.7%) and Dorval (19.1%). In most municipalities, Black was the largest visible minority group, followed by Arab or Latin American. But Chinese and South Asian were the largest visible minority groups in Brossard, Pointe-Claire and Kirkland.

While Montréal is, by far, the most multicultural part of Québec, at 16.5% it has the second lowest proportion of visible minorities of Canada's six biggest cities. (Toronto 42.9%, Vancouver 41.7%, Calgary 22.2%, Edmonton 17.1%, Ottawa-Gatineau 16%.) Perhaps this is one of the reasons that Québec seems to be having the hardest time with immigrants "fitting in." Montréal is a city complicated by 240 years of language conflict, which makes it unique in Canada. Immigrants get caught in the complicated web of French-English competition and both sides use them as pawns in Canada's longest-running chess game. French-speaking Québecers also have the strongest sense of self-identity (perhaps tied with Newfoundlanders), which, ironically, may work against immigrants easily fitting in. The notion of "accommodation" looks much different in a place with clearly defined cultural norms (and where those norms were a defence against a ruling elite that tried to crush the majority) compared to one where the notion of being Canadian always seemed slightly out of focus.

Whatever the reason, Québec has had a harder time than the rest of Canada in being comfortable with newcomers. But a walk in Montréal demonstrates that young people there are like young people across Canada. Anyone who visits its streets, Metro, schoolyards and ice rinks will see that, like the rest of the country, most young people feel comfortable with the only reality they have known: Their friends, classmates, teammates, teachers, neighbours and familiar strangers look like people from every corner of the planet. Most Montréalers, like most Canadians, are proud of the new culture we are creating.

The older I get the more my favourite pets are peeves. Like the designated hitter and aluminum bats, which brought on steroids and wrecked baseball. Or cable TV with a hundred channels, but not one damn interesting program on. Truth is that TV is all about selling. It is one part entertainment, half part information, half part intellectual stimulation and eight parts advertising. Our world is consumed by buying. Buying is the solution to loneliness. Buying will get you a guy. Buying will make you more of a man. Buying will turn around the lousy economy. Buying will even help the environment. We watch and we believe and that's how the system enslaves us. Wanting more stuff and debt from the previous stuff we were convinced to buy chain us to our boring, shitty jobs. We're stuck, addicted to the system. Addicted to capitalism. But you know what? The first step in beating an addiction is taking personal responsibility for quitting.

# CHAPTER 5

# The new Canadian dream

Just like hockey has changed over the decades as players became bigger, stronger and faster through better nutrition and conditioning, so too has Canada as the players on our team have become more diverse. As the previous chapter suggests, perhaps we have so much difficulty coming up with an answer to "What is a Canadian?" because it is a moving target. Instead, we need to be asking: "Who is becoming Canadian?" and "Who are Canadians becoming?" These suggest more questions: "Where is this all headed?" and "Do we like who we are becoming?" and "What can we do to influence the outcome?"

Of course there is still a significant minority that has not come to terms with the past few decades of Canadian immigration policy. For them, the questions remain: "Is immigration a good or a bad thing?" and (let's be honest here) "How many of those damn foreigners are they going to allow into our country?" Many of us avoid discussing immigration because the conversation invites the screamers among that minority to shout insults from the standing room areas at the top of the arena. But, unlike the crazies at the hockey rink, these ones can do real damage with their racism, xenophobia and just plain meanness.

Still, it's not necessarily racist or anti-immigrant to ask: Who is coming to our country? Why should we accept levels of immigration that change the cultural and ethnic makeup of our country? We're giving up part of our identity and what's in it for us in return? Is immigration good for ordinary Canadians or just for our economic elites? Why should ordinary Canadians think mass immigration is a good idea? For every argument that newcomers are good for the economy there is another that says workers should worry about immigrants competing for jobs and driving wages down, especially with the economy in recession. For every 10 people who like the changing ethnic landscape there's three who want things to remain the way they remember it used to be.

The truth is, it's still remarkably easy to whip up anti-immigrant hysteria in many quarters. Some of us feel like victims of change. We had no input into the process that decided all these strange looking people from around the world could come to our country, province, city, town and neighbourhood.

If we simply look to the past for what it means to be Canadian then we have good reason to be fearful of these newcomers. We see our world changing and that makes us uncomfortable. Strangers seem a threat. Why? Because there is no vision of where these changes are taking us. And when we ask "what's in it for us?" no one answers, except the voices of negativity, the racists and those who are stuck in the past. The best the defenders of immigration usually come up with is "it's good for the economy," which was fine until the economic crisis came along and unemployment rose. What's in it for us under these circumstances?

There is a good answer. It should have been obvious, but no one has spoken up about it before. Perhaps, because of our tendency towards conservative solutions, we have overlooked the readily apparent, groundbreaking project available to us: Canada has acquired the potential, through immigration over the past 40 years, to become the first nation to have a population representative of the entire world.

Stop and think about that for a moment. Canada could be the first place ever to have a single government that is a representative sample of the entire planet's population. Remember the song We Are the World? It could be about us.

In fact, we are well on our way. Let's repeat a paragraph from the previous chapter: Canada attracts new citizens from every ethnic group and all corners of the world. Of the 1.2 million immigrants who arrived between 2001 and 2006, 58% came from Asia, including the Middle East; 16% from Europe; 11% from the Caribbean, Central and South America; 10.5% from Africa; and 3.5% from the United States. Compare that to a planet where about 61% of the population is Asian, 12% is European, 13% African, 9% from South America and the Caribbean, and 5% North American. We are almost the world and becoming more and more like it every year.

Where is this leading us? To put it in genetic terms, we could be the first place on Earth to have a representative sample of the entire diversity of human DNA. To put it in anthropological terms, when we have a truly representative sample of all the world's peoples, we will have no choice but to figure out ways of getting along and interacting with each other, which will make Canada humanity's first real melting pot. This country could be truly international, truly human and a beacon for the planet. To put it in economic terms, if we had direct family and other people-to-people connections with every corner of the globe, Canada could become a model for true free trade, not simply another rich and powerful country that uses the term to mask the reality of colonial relationships. To put it in cultural terms, if we have artists from every corner of the planet, we could develop music, art, writing, film and other forms of expression that truly reflect all of humanity. Canadian music would become distinct by fusing sounds from every corner of the world; our visual arts too by exposure to the traditions our immigrants bring with them; our films could explore the entire world inside Canada; our writers would be a voice to explain our world to the world. To put it in sporting terms, we could field teams among the best in the world in whatever sport we care to by making Canada home to the widest possible range of human physical types and attracting the best coaches from every corner of the planet. We could rule the world! Or at least win a few more gold medals at the Olympics.

If we continue to attract immigrants from every corner of the planet eventually Canada's "ethnicity" will become "human" rather than English, or French, or European. Multiculturalism will still allow individuals to value their hyphenated identity, if they so choose, but as our country becomes more and more diverse "Canadian" will transcend all current notions of ethnicity.

The cultural, intellectual and economic result of becoming the planet's first country whose ethnicity was "human" would certainly put us in the world spotlight. Canada would have the opportunity to lead our planet past old ethnic and "racial" divisions, to a planetary culture, an ideology of common humanity and an international economy that serves the entire Earth and all the creatures on it.

What might such a Canada look like? How would its people and government act? What might an ideology of common humanity be like?

We can get a glimpse of this new Canada at St. Clair and Bathurst in Toronto or the Metrotown Mall in the Vancouver suburb of Burnaby or dozens of other locations in our biggest cities. When the children of people who were born in India, Uganda, Romania, China, the United States, Brazil, the Philippines, Ireland, Nigeria, Lebanon, Germany, Bolivia, Russia, El Salvador, Pakistan, Indonesia and Canada interact they see neighbours, co-workers, fellow Canadians and friends. The other kids in their schools were from all those countries and more. It's the people they are used to. They see us, rather than them. Their circle includes the whole world. Their sense of being Canadian includes people whose ethnic origins are everywhere in the world.

Even those of us past the age of 50, who grew up in a much different Canada, now must listen to a person's accent before asking "where are you from?" Judging a person by their "look" all too often proves embarrassing. Instead of the anticipated answer of "Hong Kong" or "India" we get "I grew up in east Vancouver, how about you?" or "I'm from Scarborough, why do you ask?" As time goes by, we become accustomed to the wider variety of "looks" and eventually that is just what Toronto or Vancouver or Montréal or Calgary or Canada is like. This pan-planet ethnicity becomes who we are, who we see as us. Most Canadians are proud of being "not racist" and "diverse" even though it is not always true. Our diversity has produced an ideology of multiculturalism that is evolving into something more. With the right policies it could evolve into something very important for Canada and the world.

With a population that is more and more representative of the entire planet, Canada has the opportunity to develop a nationalism that is post-ethnic, democratic and internationalist. That would certainly make us a beacon to the world. In fact, post-ethnic, democratic, internationalist nationalism is exactly what the world needs, and soon. Human beings have used education, science, economics and technology to create weapons powerful enough to destroy the planet — many would say we are destroying it already through global warming and pollution — but so far we have not developed a pan-ethnic, pan-national culture as a foundation on which to build the economic and political structures necessary to harness our power. But we must, if we are to live in harmony with each other and nature.

Of course an ideology of common humanity would not automatically arise from a Canada that contained a representative sample of all the world's people. We would have established the possibility, perhaps even the necessity, for this ideology, but its creation would not be guaranteed. Enough of us must still want to believe in such a world-view and consciously convince others that it makes sense.

There is another possible result of having people of different ethnic and religious backgrounds living in the same cities and regions. They can form ghettos and develop ideologies of us and them, of being better than others, of ethnic and religious rivalries. These divisions can lead to dysfunctional and weak governments. These divisions can be manipulated by elites, here or abroad, to divide and conquer Canadians, to keep us fighting with each other, rather than building a great country. This is nothing new. In fact, this is how most empires have kept economic, military and political power in the hands of powerful minorities.

So, as we continue along our path of mass immigration from every part of the planet, these are two ends of the spectrum of possible outcomes: A weak, unimportant society divided into ethnic and religious ghettos that fight each other for power in which a small elite (foreign or domestic) uses those divisions as a form of divide and conquer; Or a self-confident society that develops a pan-ethnic, pan-national, democratic "nationalism" that is a beacon to all those who seek to build a better world.

I know which way my vote will be cast and that will be for the Canadian way.

The people on this land have compromised, accommodated and learned to live together throughout Canada's history. Post-ethnic, democratic, internationalist nationalism is simply the logical outcome of that.

What could possibly be a better vision for Canada? What's on offer? To continue being a junior partner to the USA? That road ultimately leads to assimilation and the end of the Canadian dream. Given this country's location and climate, we're unlikely to become the most populous country in the world. For the same reason we'll never be the most powerful nation. Perhaps we could be the wealthiest people in the world, but that seems a rather shallow ambition, compared to leading the world past old ethnic and national divisions that have caused so much suffering. There is a desperate need for a country that can balance the environmental and economic, which sees itself as one with the entire planet, and all the people on it. We already have too many places where the production of ever more products is the sole measure of success.

But can Canadians really aspire to such greatness? We're a modest nation, with self-effacing people (except during the Stanley Cup playoffs). We've never been important and certainly have never been recognized as a world leader in much beyond hockey. We've never strutted on the world stage or proclaimed any sort of manifest destiny. No one would describe us as one of the world's powerful nations.

And that is precisely why Canada is the perfect country to build a post-ethnic, democratic, internationalist nationalism. We do not threaten the more powerful nations of the world. It can work here in the northern half of North America because we are not and likely never will be a great power.

And, if the world is to have any future, the most powerful country must learn that it is better to cooperate than to dominate. Canada, with all its close southern ties, is also best situated to play the role of teacher to our closest neighbour.

But some might argue that "post-ethnic, democratic, internationalist nationalism" is an oxymoron. Theirs would be superficial reasoning. While a sense of belonging to a group is a basic human need, all of us (except psychopaths or other severely damaged individuals) belong to overlapping concentric circles of communities that include some or all of: family, kinship group, friendship network, team, neighbourhood, town or city, province or state, nation, ethnic group, class, language, religion, politics. Nationalism is simply one circle of community, another sense of belonging. Of course nationalism has been abused in the past (and today) to build empires or to justify stealing from others, but so have family, religion, ethnicity and all our other feelings of community. The danger is not our sense of belonging to a nation or to an ethnic group, but rather our lack of a sense of community as a common humanity, or as a living thing, or as a part of the planet, or as an integral part of the universe. We need to expand our circle.

The process we must encourage is one that creates these additional feelings of belonging. Just as most of today's nationalisms were created and consciously built during the 19th and 20th centuries, in the new millennium we need to engage in a similar process for post-ethnic internationalism. Canada, with the help of millions of new immigrants, could be the first place to make it happen.

Or is this notion too pie in the sky? Let's consider what would be required for the goal to be achieved. How difficult a path would it be from where we are today to the place we want to go? Would it involve a radical break from our past?

The reality is that Canada has been headed on the path described for its entire history, but especially for the past 35 years. People from every country, every ethnic group, every culture around the planet have become citizens, have learned to live with each other and are building a new Canadian identity that is more and more multicultural, international and pan-human. Our ideas are slowly beginning to reflect who we are becoming. The desire for Canada to be an economic and social force for good around the world grows every day. Creating a post-ethnic, democratic, internationalist nationalism is not pie in the sky, but rather it is already happening. Or at least the possibility of it happening has been happening. We have simply lacked self-awareness.

Building an international, post-ethnic, human culture does not mean denying the importance of the places where we live, or the past that has created us. It means building on who we have been and striving for more. All nationalisms — English, German, French, Indian, Mexican, Chinese, South African, Serbian, Ethiopian, etc. — have been creations of something greater than simple history or everyday experience. They have been rallying cries for building empires, or defending territory or defining a people's place in a threatening world. Artists, politicians, intellectuals and ordinary citizens built these nationalisms through a conscious process of creating myths that make sense based on shared experiences. In the same fashion, an international, post-ethnic, human culture could be built from shared experiences and a conscious building process. This can only happen in the communities where we live. Or to borrow and twist an idea, we must learn to think globally, but create our culture locally.

Just as we have been doing, we need to welcome people from around the world into our communities and then work with them to create this new post-ethnic, democratic, internationalist nationalism. It is not an exact thing that we can define beforehand. Rather this new culture will be a result of the process of newcomers and current Canadians reacting to each other.

Or course, we do need to think about how this process might work and how to manage it. The suggestions of one proud Canadian follow.

You know another thing that makes me want to throw a glass at the damn flat-screen TV? Every time some asshole commentator says "west" when he really means Alberta. Like, the West is conservative. Well, goddamn it, the West just happens to be the part of Canada that elected 90% of all the NDP-CCF governments in the history of this country. The big cities in Manitoba, Saskatchewan and B.C. are the most left-wing places in Canada, electing socialists going back to before the First World War. The West is conservative like the Rocky Mountains go all the way to Vancouver!

# CHAPTER 6

# The right sort of immigrant

If, through immigration, we are going to build the world's first post-ethnic, internationalist nationalism, a question to be asked is what sort of newcomers would facilitate this? Those who choose to come here is one obvious answer, but not a good enough one. While a desire to become Canadian is a necessary first step, it is often not sufficient for becoming a successful immigrant. You must also fit in.

What this means is the subject of a debate much older than Canada itself. Who should be allowed/encouraged to be a Canadian is the same question that has been asked since much of what is now Canada was a French colony. Do we want soldiers? Farmers? Perhaps we should send over criminals. When the British took over: Should we encourage farmers? Do we give land to soldiers who have done their duty? Can we trust the Irish? Are American settlers a Fifth Column? Where do First Nations fit in?

The debate over immigration has always been bound by the goals of the debaters. When the object was to create a loyal pink bit on the map of the British Empire that goal determined the criteria used to judge potential immigrants. When the British Empire disintegrated, the object became more purely economic and the criteria used to judge immigrants shifted. Ethnicity and country of origin became less important. Job skills and education replaced potential loyalty to the monarch. But the bottom line has always been applying some criteria by which we judge potential immigrants.

It's okay for us to expect, even demand, some things from the newcomers who want to live in our country. Hell, we expect and demand things from people who were born here so why not from people who weren't? Like when a cooperative housing board interviews potential new residents and has a list of the ideal qualities by which to judge them, it is fair for Canada to come up with criteria to evaluate potential immigrants. Unfortunately, the details can bedevil us.

There are still some Canadians who would prefer only white British, American, Australian, South African and New Zealanders be allowed into our country. Others would widen the criteria to anyone of a European background. Fortunately, only a small and shrinking minority holds such racist attitudes. Others would limit immigration to highly skilled or wealthy immigrants, arguing that immigrants should directly add something to our economy. Many of us, however, believe that when such immigrants come from poor countries this is just another form of colonialism, a way of pillaging countries that need the resources more than us. Many recent citizens argue that family reunification should be part of the criteria for selecting immigrants. Still others say we should bring in immigrants who are willing to do the worst jobs, often at lousy pay, and then send them packing when we don't need them anymore.

Of course Canada's current immigration system does

favour certain kinds of immigrants. That's what the point system is all about. Education, age, skills, experience, size of bank account and family connections are all factors considered by the bureaucracy that determines who gets in. All these are useful because they are in some sense quantifiable, which makes them "objective" in a bureaucratic sense. But there are other criteria, at least as important, which are not quantifiable and a point system, or other sorts of regulations, can never capture. They have to do with "fitting in" and helping Canada become the "kind of place" we want it to be. Of course, this is a difficult topic with as many opinions as there are political points of view. The kind of place you want Canada to be determines your answer to the question: Who is an ideal Canadian? And one's response to that is directly connected to what sort of immigrant you believe would best fit in.

One way to answer this question is to consider the "point" of being Canadian. From a historical perspective, as I have argued above, this has always primarily been "to not be American" or to "be better than Americans." For those of us who agree, an ideal Canadian is one who shares this perspective. Therefore we should encourage immigrants who would accentuate our differences with the USA and help Canada be better than our neighbour to the south. But, what exactly might that mean?

If asked, Canadians would overwhelmingly answer that this country is better than the United States because we provide a government-run, universal medical-care system as part of a social safety net for all citizens. Most of us would say that Canada is better because we are more tolerant of differences in ethnic background, language, country of origin and sexual orientation. Most would respond that Canada is better than the USA because we prefer peace-keeping to waging war and would rather spend our taxes on social services than on the military — Canadians are proud that most people in the world do not believe us to be imperialists, unlike our neighbours to the south who are more and more seen as ugly Americans. Most of us think Canada is better than the USA because we are citizens of the world, who think all people, including foreigners, have rights. A majority would agree that Canada is better because our income disparities are less, we are more egalitarian, and we use our taxation, social welfare and education systems to promote equality of opportunity. Finally, we overwhelmingly prefer Canada's social welfare economic system to the USA's naked capitalism. For example one recent poll had 87% of Canadians preferring our socialized medical care system compared to only 7% liking the U.S. private model.

In other words, most of us, including supporters of the Liberals, Bloc Québecois and even the Conservatives, think Canada's "socialism" makes our country better than the USA. We prefer to be politically "to the left" of the United States. It's difficult to imagine a single area where even a significant minority of Canadians would say we are better than the USA because we are more right wing.

Of course, some Canadians would say the USA is better than us because it is more capitalistic, more religious, more law-and-order oriented, more war-like, more powerful, or more right-wing, but they are a minority. Of course some of these people are rich and powerful (or sycophants thereof) who only care about their narrow self-interest, who deny there is any such thing as the common good and who spend large sums of money to confuse the rest of us. They seem to believe that the best way for them to become even wealthier is for Canada to tie itself ever more closely to the USA. Fortunately most Canadians, who have witnessed the ill effects of extreme laissez-faire capitalism south of the border, don't fall for their propaganda. If we wanted to be like Americans we would move there and some of us do. We understand that we live next to the most powerful nation in the world and anything we do must take that fact into account. But, rather than be the sort of neighbour who keeps up with the Joneses by blindly copying everything they do, we prefer to be the independent, friendly family next door who has their own sense of style and their own way of doing things. We believe that makes the world a much more interesting neighbourhood in which to live.

The kind of country most of us prefer is clear, but what sort of immigrants would assist Canada in remaining "to the left" of the United States? What criteria could we come up with to judge whether or not newcomers might strengthen Canada's social welfare system? Is there a connection between the immigrants who come here and our ongoing relationship with the rest of the world? If we accept more immigrants with a certain background will that make Canada less likely to become a warmongering imperial power? If we let too many immigrants of one kind into our country do we risk becoming more "capitalistic" and therefore too much like the United States? Is there a balance of kinds of immigrants that we need in order to be the sort of country most of us prefer?

These are complicated questions with no easy answers, but one thing is perfectly clear: One sort of immigrant should be discouraged. If a key element in our immigration policy is to help Canada be distinctive, to be better than the United States, then we don't want people for whom this country is a second choice, who really want to become American and dream of the day they will win the U.S. immigration lottery. Unfortunately this sort of immigrant has a long history in our country. Millions of newcomers over the decades have used Canada as a stepping-stone to the United States. Even today one can enter a restaurant or a store run by someone who recently entered the country under the investor-entrepreneur program and find the television tuned to a U.S. news channel. What does that say about fitting into Canadian society?

The absolute minimum we should ask of immigrants is a commitment to Canada as a distinct country and this commitment should be positive, rather than negative. By this I mean, anti-Americanism is not what we want, but rather a dedication to the positive goals of Canada's distinctiveness. We want immigrants who place a high value on defending and extending our social safety net, who believe in peacekeeping over making war, who relish the fact that Canada is both French and English and owes a great debt to our First Nations, who embrace diversity, who are internationalists not imperialists, who want to be part of a community that helps people in their times of need and doesn't allow great disparities in income or wealth. These are not "anti-American" values. In fact, many of our neighbours to the south would say these are values they share.

This raises an ironic point: One important source for the sort of immigrants that would help Canada remain an independent, distinctive nation is the country we wish to remain distinctive from. There is every reason to believe that more Americans share the "Canadian values" outlined above than the entire population of Canada. With over 300 million citizens, even if only a quarter of Americans share the values of internationalism, anti-imperialism, tolerance of diversity and enhanced social welfare systems, that is much more than double the population of Canada. In fact, this country has for decades attracted immigrants from the United States who were fleeing McCarthyism, homophobia, religious intolerance, the war in Vietnam, a private-for-profit medical care system and George W. Bush.

The best bet would be to arrange a trade with Aunt Samantha. She takes all our right-wing, fundamentalist, neo-conservative, authoritarian, racist, or money-seeking citizens while we get all her left-liberal types. You think Samantha would agree?

Seriously though, many of our U.S. friends see Canada as an alternative, a beacon of left-liberal hope. We are close enough to their culture to be familiar, but not so dominated by economic and religious fundamentalism. We need to build on this strength of the Canadian "brand" to attract these newcomers, who fit in easily and bring with them a strong commitment to the values we share. Attracting well-educated, skilled, relatively wealthy immigrants from the USA also avoids the problem, raised above, of stealing the precious human resources of poorer countries.

The idea of "branding" Canada as the left-wing alternative to the USA's hyper-capitalism has, sadly, been mostly ignored by our government and corporations, but universities, hospitals, other institutions and even some small businesses have attracted people from across the border by just such an approach. So far this has been low key and unorganized, but there is a very large pool of progressive Americans who could be targeted as one of Canada's niche markets for immigrants. This country already has brand strength in the U.S. liberal market, mostly as a legacy from draft dodgers and other war resisters during the American war in Southeast Asia. The fact that Canada refused to overtly participate in the Iraq war debacle further improved this country's attractiveness. If our governments created marketing campaigns targeting the tens of millions of American liberals, and those further left, who are physicians, plumbers, scientists, electricians, social workers, welders, teachers, mechanics, nurses, carpenters and others we could easily solve all our skilled-worker shortages, at least in English-speaking Canada. (There are also millions of U.S. citizens of French-Canadian background who could be a niche immigrant market for Québec. Think of all the jobs teaching them how to speak French.) And we would strengthen our core progressive values at the same time. The legacy of immigration from the U.S. in the 1960s and '70s

— tens of thousands of draft dodgers and deserters became productive Canadians — as a result of the American war in Southeast Asia proves this could be a successful strategy.

Targeting liberal and other dissident niche markets for immigrants could be applied to other countries as well. People who rebel against repression and become targets of their own government are often exactly the kind of people who make ideal Canadians. For example, this country gained hundreds of thousands of excellent citizens when people from Chile, Guatemala, Iran, El Salvador, Haiti, Vietnam, Uganda, Greece, Hungary, Algeria, Czechoslovakia, Syria, Palestine and other countries fled political persecution and upheaval in their homelands. There are many reasons to believe that political upheaval and persecution will be with us for some time, so refugees will continue to be an important source of new Canadians.

But, some would argue, refugees don't bring resources, are sometimes not well educated and require resettlement programs that are expensive and raise our taxes. This argument is an example of short-term thinking. Accepting, even encouraging, refugees is an investment in Canada's future. Typical characteristics of refugees are the spirit of independence and a willingness to fight for what one thinks is right. These are more important than job skills or money. Refugees are motivated and creative; they must be in order to survive. It's difficult to leave one's home; the easy way is to accept the status quo and stay where you are. Refugees are the people who do not simply accept whatever is offered them. They leave rather than accept their fate. This is a prime indicator of potential creativity and that should be the No. 1 requirement for immigrants to Canada. If we are to break away from our economic, cultural and social dependence on the USA and become a model of a better way for the rest of the world, a great deal of creativity will be required. Any help we can get from immigrants would be like having the new kid, who joins the atom team just after the season starts, turn out to be a top goal scorer.

Other arguments in favour of accepting refugees are that offering a place to people without homes is the humanitarian (which should be interchangeable with the "Canadian") thing to do and that doing so also furthers the process of this country becoming more multicultural and internationalist. And these are two of the distinguishing features of Canada that need to be strengthened if we are to reach our potential of building the world's first post-ethnic, democratic, internationalist nationalism. Refugees from all corners of the planet are clearly a necessary element to ensure the success of this project.

There would be no need for a radical shift in Canada's immigration policy. We already do accept refugees and the numbers could be adjusted upwards over time. There would also be no need to make major changes to our family reunification policies. Provided that family members who come to Canada are willing to accept our post-ethnic, democratic, internationalist nationalism, it makes sense to accept people who can take advantage of pre-existing social support networks. Perhaps only in the area of the "points system" would significant changes be required to align our current immigration policies with the new Canadian post-ethnic, democratic, internationalist nationalism. This would most likely involve the de-emphasis of points for particular job skills to be replaced by some sort of criteria that would focus on making sure Canada was becoming more and more representative of all the world's people.

What we need to do now is continue on the immigration path we have been following but become explicit about the project we are embarked on. We need to tell potential immigrants about our post-ethnic, democratic, internationalist project and require that they work with us on it. A willingness to help build a nation whose people are self-consciously also citizens of the world and representative of all humanity should be the minimum requirement for all immigrants to Canada. Our most favoured immigrants should be ones who can demonstrate a passion for this vision of Canada, no matter their wealth, education or job skills.

Of course, we should never forget what it is that got us here. We must also ask immigrants to be passionate about the other Canadian traits that we wish to promote. They should be passionately polite, passionately hate referees and passionately love hockey. They should be passionately funny, or at least willing to laugh at themselves. They should be passionate about language — theirs and ours and as many others as they can learn — and willing to make a commitment that their children will learn both French and English.

But most important of all, immigrants must understand that while Canadians, from coast to coast to coast to the invisible line that separates us from the USA, respect fair play, we also like at least one dirty guy on our side. So, you new guys better always skate with your head up and never show fear when going into a corner. And whatever happens shake hands when the game is over so you can leave the rink laughing. Translated from hockey talk this means every immigrant should be prepared for something bad to happen, because not everyone will like you. Work hard, stand up for yourself and don't let anyone intimidate you, but also don't take things too seriously and, no matter what, try to make friends with everyone by having a good sense of humour.

Which brings up the important subject of "Canadian" values.

Another thing that tightens my sphincter and gets the blood vessels on the side of my head popping is ignorant generalizations. That's what prejudice is. People say or believe things about people they don't know that they wouldn't possibly believe about people they actually know. Few people would claim that "everyone on my block is good at math" because it just wouldn't make sense. We know that some people on our block may be good at math but others are not. Yet some people are prepared to believe that certain large groups of people are lazy or others are cheap or these people are good at mathematics or those guys are greedy or some other stupid stereotype. And even worse, racists take advantage of ignorant generalizations to divide us and do harm. I say stop racism. Think before you buy into an ignorant generalization.

# CHAPTER 7

# A Team Canada philosophy

As discussed in the previous chapter, who might make the best sort of immigrant to build our post-ethnic internationalist nationalism cannot be defined too narrowly, but rather the point is to manage what happens when people from all parts of the planet come together in one place. In the same way, any new ideology of what it means to be Canadian must be developed over time as a response to this diversity. Ideology flows from what is actually happening.

But, if we are to embark on this project we must give some thought to what sort of ideas would best go along with being post-ethnic, internationalist and yet still be Canadian. When we request of immigrants that they accept certain values as part of the process of becoming Canadian, we must give them at least some vague outline of what those values should be. When we tell immigrants that they must learn to act Canadian, we should offer some clues as to what that means. To put it in hockey terms: Every Stanley Cup winner has a team philosophy out of which flows the various game plans that ensure success.

If we want to lead the world by building a post-ethnic, internationalist, democratic nationalism, our team philosophy must be to promote a common humanity, stress cooperation in addition to healthy competition, and seek to solve problems by compromise rather than force. Our game plan must be to put those principles into action. The key to moving beyond vague positive feelings about multiculturalism and claiming to be "a force for good in the world" is developing a "Team Canada" philosophy. We must come up with a set of principles that define who we are striving to be and the standards by which we judge our actions. These principles must make sense to both prospective immigrants and multi-generation Canadians. They must attract new immigrants and unite current Canadians in an exciting project to build the world's best country. These principles are the foundation of the Team Canada philosophy.

Like any good team philosophy it must take into account the skills and talents of the team; it must make sense, both individually and collectively, to the players; and it must be repeated over and over until it become part of the players' unconscious belief system. The team philosophy and the game plan flowing out of it needs to be practical, based on hard work and reality, not a utopian fantasy. Experience tells us that if we can't see on a map how to get from where we are to where we want to go, we're probably lost.

The object is to create a widespread belief that to be a good Canadian is also to be a good citizen of the world. This requires ideas and actions that will unite us, not divide us, and that express our common humanity. They must be ideas and actions that make sense to people from a wide range of political, cultural and religious backgrounds. They must reflect our collective experience and the language of these ideas and actions must also be one that the vast majority of us understand.

What follows are the suggestions of one Canadian, who understands the process will require the creativity of millions. Feel free to criticize, to express outrage, to pooh pooh, and to offer your own, better views. Engagement in the process is the goal.

So, who is an ideal Canadian for building a post-ethnic, internationalist, democratic nationalism? For me, an ideal Canadian is one who believes:

**Do unto other people and countries, as you would have them do unto you.** While variations on the golden rule exist in almost every religion and belief system, it has been strikingly absent from international affairs. Instead, the history of foreign relations has been one of war and plunder, at worst, or unequal power and interference, at best. But just because that's the way things have been does not mean that's how they must be. If, inside Canada, a proportion of Ontario taxes can go to help less developed provinces, why can't the same sort of thing be done on a world scale? The problem is not an absence of mechanisms that could work, but rather, our attitude has been one of extreme competition and "screw thy neighbour" rather than cooperation and mutual aid. Too often we have justified exploitation and other forms of dehumanization by perverse economic or even religious theories. An ideal Canadian speaks up to protest when this occurs.

**He who plays in a glass hockey rink should be careful how hard he shoots the puck.** This is also known as judge thyself before judging others. Or, don't be a hypocrite. Canadians know that nothing more quickly undermines the goodwill necessary to maintain a fractious federal system than not playing fair. Rules must apply to the most powerful and to the weakest. If a few big kids hog the puck and break all the rules in a pick-up hockey game, eventually everyone else stops playing. The best way to make sure the game is played fairly is for each of us to call penalties on ourselves. An ideal Canadian understands that winning doesn't count if you cheat. Translated into the arena of international affairs, this means every country, not just the weak ones, must be subject to the same rules. Only after a president of the most powerful country in the world is found guilty of starting an illegal war and pays for his crime will the rules of the game be perceived as fair by all. Only when the best player on the ice follows the rules will there be any chance of a good game.

**Look out for your neighbours.** This is something that almost everybody, everywhere does sometimes. It is especially acted upon during times when we have no choice but to rely on cooperation and helping each other. It is often not commented upon in big cities, except during storms or disasters such as earthquakes, but it is a daily fact of life in many rural communities. We can choose to think of the entire planet as our village. In the context of an infinite universe the Earth is the equivalent of a Newfoundland outport where people as a matter of course get together to rebuild their neighbour's house after a fire. Since Canadians have friends and family in every corner of the world, we must treat them all as if they were part of our village. This means a push when their car gets stuck, help to raise a new barn when one burns down, patronizing their new business to help them get started and the thousands of other ways to be a good neighbour. Ideal Canadians believe that people in every corner of the globe are our neighbours.

**There is no such thing as race.** There is simply no biological or genetic basis for the claim, which most of us learned from our parents, that people can be divided up into groups such as white, black, brown, yellow, red, European, African, Asian, etc., or any other such notion. The only reality that race has ever had is as a social category that has been used for centuries to justify privileges for some members of humanity. The only reason to use the idea of race nowadays should be to discuss how to rectify the wrongs of the past. For example, the old categories of race must be applied if we are to understand what was done to First Nations or to the descendents of African slaves, and to overcome the damage that racism caused. In other words, you can't fix a problem that, in part, was caused by an idea, by simply pretending the idea never existed. Ideal Canadians understand the ways privilege and injustice have been justified and are prepared to do what is necessary to right historical wrongs so that everyone has a fair chance.

**We are all Africans.** Scientists have discovered that every human being shares common ancestors, who theoretically can be traced right back to a single mother in Africa. This is an important idea because it gives a solid foundation to the widening of our circles of belonging to include all of humanity. Ideal Canadians believe all people are members of one big family.

**We are individuals and team players at the same time.** This is an important truth that we learn particularly well from hockey. The greatest players are the ones who make their teammates better, not those who have the best individual skills. In hockey the best lines are the ones that are greater than the sum of three individual players. Perhaps this is one reason we are more of a collectivist society than the USA, where individualism has run rampant. While wanting to be the best you can be is important, it is not enough to create a truly great team. Doing what it takes to make others better is also something we all must do. We win with the right balance of team and individual play. Ideal Canadians understand that, as individuals, our job is not only to be the best we can be, but also to help our teammates, who — in the big picture — are everyone and everything, be the best they can be.

**We are all the same and we are all different.** More than one thing defines us. We can be a Canadian and a Québecer. We can be Ukrainian-Canadian or a just plain Canadian. We can have interests as a woman and as a Canadian. There's a time to stress differences and a time to stress similarities. Canadians have long experience with duality and multiplicity. While some might argue that stressing our differences weakens our resolve, it in fact gives us one of our greatest strengths, diversity. With an understanding that reality is diverse comes wisdom. Because we are more than one thing we are tolerant of differences. Tolerance allows us to get along. Our diversity, wisdom, tolerance and ability to get along are the keys to being trusted. If we can achieve the trust of most people, we can lead the world. For a short while, the USA laid claim to leading the world, but no more. An insistence that theirs is the only way, a lack of wisdom, intolerance and the use of force to get its way have revealed to the world over the past few decades that country's shortcomings. We need to learn from their mistakes. Ideal Canadians understand that the best way to lead is by example — real leaders are people we want to emulate — and this means we never insist that others be the same as us.

**It takes an outport to raise a child.** The best citizen is one who has a sense of responsibility towards others. This sense should be the motivation for political or other community activity. The place where we gain this sense of responsibility is where we grow up. If all the people around us take care of us, we learn that taking care of each other is what we do. Sharing the responsibility of raising children has the added benefit of helping to overcome the flaws that all parents have. If we imagine our communities as a series of concentric circles, the biggest one being the entire planet, then this positive social force can encompass everyone. Ideal Canadians understand that the world is a better place if we feel some responsibility for every child on the planet.

**The rule of law is necessary, but referees get booed when they make a mistake.** This is just another way of saying the law belongs to us, rather than ruling over us. We value order, but not for its own sake. The point of rules is to create the best and most fair game possible. To ensure fairness we will change the rules. As well, we have a healthy skepticism about the enforcers of law. We do not glorify referees and they are not the heroes of our game. They are necessary and even deserving of respect, but they are best when not noticed. The job of the referee is to make sure the game is played fairly. The point of the rule of law is to ensure fairness and justice for all. If the law is unfair and creates injustice then it is fair game to break the rules. It's more important to do what is right than to blindly follow orders. A fundamental difference between Canada and the United States is that we have the two-minute penalty, while they have capital punishment. Ideal Canadians respect the law but understand its limits and know that referees make mistakes.

Who is an ideal Canadian? An ideal Canadian is one who:

**Celebrates every culture.** The real genius of Canada's multiculturalism policy is that while it defines a successful immigrant as someone who adds to our culture, it also asserts that a good Canadian is someone who is willing to accept differences and change. The reason multiculturalism has worked better in Canada than in other countries is because the question of who we are has always been so difficult to answer. We've been willing to accept others because we have never been certain who we are, so how could we think we were better than anyone? The meaning of being Canadian is so fluid that we have been able to successfully accommodate high levels of immigration. And this is a self-reinforcing process: The more it works, the better it works and the more it works. Ideal Canadians are willing and eager to learn from every culture because they understand that diversity brings wisdom and strength.

**Plays hard but shakes hands when the game is over.** It's okay to compete, to defeat your opponent in a game, but ultimately we are all players and must respect each other. Someone who skated against you today could be skating with you tomorrow. This is the difference between an opponent and an enemy. The Canadian way is to understand that no one is your enemy, but rather opponents in a particular game. We have learned that not only in childhood shinny games, but also in our country's relationship with the United States. We can dislike their government, we can hate the things their military industrial complex does, we can make fun of their politics and religion, but they are still our closest neighbours and we do like many things about them. Ideal Canadians understand that no one is an enemy but that everyone can one day be on the other team.

**Lives in harmony with the environment.** Our First Nations survived for millennia by learning to thrive with the environment, not against it. Then the immigrants who were our European and other forbearers came along to conquer both the people and the land. Canada's current immigrants must not repeat this destructive attitude. Rather than raping and pillaging the environment we must imagine a symbiosis. We must strive to create a balance of our needs with those of the rest of the planet. Ideal Canadians believe, like our First Nations ancestors, the earth is our mother and everything on it is related to us.

**Plays fair and clean, but is always willing to drop his**

**gloves.** A good Canadian is a pacifist who is willing to fight for peace. A truth one learns as a kid playing pick-up hockey on outdoor ice is that the only thing worse than a bully picking on you is not standing up to that bully. If this country is to lead the world, it must be prepared to stand up to bullies. This is especially important when the bully is close to us. We teach our children that real leaders don't go along with bad stuff, even when the biggest, toughest kid on the block, who claims to be our friend, is doing it. Ideal Canadians speak truth to power and don't let anyone pick on us, or our teammates — and our teammates are everybody. Ideal Canadians choose to do what is right, not simply what the powerful tell us to do.

Any list of what makes an ideal Canadian is a work in progress. Being an ideal Canadian also means coming up with more ways of being an ideal Canadian. The critical point is that the elements of culture we want to stress and encourage new Canadians to share are those that build on our past and that help make this the best place in the world.

In the past, some of us have simply wanted to be like the United States. Others have wanted us to not be the United States. The best of us have aspired to being better than the USA. Certainly, potential immigrants who like the rugged individualistic attitudes of the stereotypical American should choose their country, not ours. Potential immigrants who admire the might of the world's most powerful military should go to the USA, not Canada. Potential immigrants who believe in competition not cooperation will be better off going to a country where that philosophy is most widely shared.

But an ideal Canadian aspires to being much more than simply better than our neighbours. An ideal Canadian wants us to be the best we can be. He believes that will make us the best in the world. An ideal Canadian believes in our potential to be the one country that everyone on the planet can count on to always be fair, kind, generous, funny and willing to live by the golden rule. Be scared to go in the corners with us, but understand that we always shake hands when the game is over.

You know what pisses me off most of all? The price of tickets to a friggin NHL game. Remember when a decent seat cost about what a union worker made in an hour? Nowadays? Double, triple or even more. It's all about tax write-offs. Teams set their prices based on what they can charge a law firm or a big corporation, which deduct 'entertainment' expenses on their tax return. Bad enough the neoliberalcons cut tax rates for the rich, but the working class also has to subsidize their season tickets and that drives up prices so high us ordinary Joes get stuck watching our game on the boob tube.

# CHAPTER 8

# Does Canada really matter?

Well, you say, this dream of post-ethnic, democratic, internationalist nationalism, may sound interesting, but it is nothing but pie in the sky. And make it rhubarb because that's what we'd have with our neighbours to the south if we even contemplate such a direction. Our only realistic choice is to follow the lead of the USA, not chart our own path, especially if it leads to a place that might upset the richest and most powerful in our rich and powerful neighbour. The truth is that some people in the United States, Canada and most other countries around the world own a stake in keeping the world the way it is. The companies they control make profits from the current system of inequality. So, in the game that counts we must remain on the bench until the real players say it's okay for us to hop over the boards.

It doesn't matter if Canadians are the nicest, fairest, best players on the ice, if the fix is in, if the rules are designed to favour one side over the other. The real world is not fair, not nice because the biggest, meanest bully on the block owns the referee. In the game that counts, might makes right and us sweet, kind, compassionate Canadians will get crushed by the political, military and economic strength of the United States. Americans will eat namby-pamby Canadian wimps as the half-time show during the Sugar and Spice Bowl and not even remember it by the time the whistle blows to end the football game. The best we can hope for is to be a farm team for the Yankees. Forget about competing in the same league.

The sad reality is that too many Canadians are persuaded by these arguments. Like the last half dozen little kids chosen for pick-up games, they assume the older, bigger boys will always be better players than them. But scrawny little kids do grow up and sometimes become better players than the bigger, older boys across the street. Or, the kids who cannot compete on the rink choose to play other games where size doesn't matter. Unfortunately, our ruling class has never grown out of its "the big kids are better than us" colonial, branch plant attitude.

Of course, Canadians do live next door to the country with the planet's most powerful military, where many of the world's richest and most possessive capitalists reside and whose government and corporations seem more and more to believe they are above the rule of international law. We would be poor coaches indeed if we did not prepare Team Canada for any possible high sticking, elbowing, boarding, tripping, fighting or interference by our hockey-playing cousins to the south. There is a good chance that the current management of Team USA would goon it up if we started outplaying them. But, like every hockey fan knows, the worst thing to do if that happens is to play scared.

Canadians got a close-up look at how the big guys on the American team lie, cheat and run their opponents from behind into the boards during the recent so-called debate about U.S. healthcare. Everyone knows their healthcare system provides the best care lots and lots of money can buy and too bad if you don't have any. For the majority of Americans the system sucks. But that doesn't matter because the owners of insurance, drug and other companies have gotten rich and use that wealth to buy the political system and keep their profits rolling in.

But just as Canadians built a public healthcare system, despite a doctors "strike" in Saskatchewan plus years of anti-Medicare propaganda, so too can we break free from the clutching and grabbing of the goons who will try to stop us from building a country based on Canadian principles. It won't be easy, but it can be done. We must come up with the right game plan and then stick to it. Listen to the coach when he says: Stay focused and don't let the other guys intimidate you.

So, what's our game plan, especially the part that gets us the big win despite the goons on the American team? Again, listen to the coach. We've got to play this game our way, not theirs. How do we do that? The way to figure this out is to understand where the Americans are better than us and where we can be better than them.

Clearly, the two biggest U.S. strengths are the power of their economy and their military might. They will beat us every time if we try to compete with them through war or the capitalist economic system. So, we must devise a game plan that takes this into account. Instead of competing by military force or by having our big companies try to crush their big companies, we must play a game we are good at. We should compete in the realm of ideas. Our dream of a post-ethnic, democratic internationalist nationalism is better than their idea of Manifest Destiny. If given a chance, it could easily win world public opinion. And the way to give it a chance is to present our idea in the arenas that favour our skills: comedy, music, film and other forms of culture. The Americans are pretty good in those arenas as well, but they do not possess the same overwhelming advantage that they have in capitalism and war.

The key will be to create a Canada that is truly independent. We must build an economy that Canadians control so that we avoid competing with the U.S. capitalists and so that we can use our resources to unleash our comedians, writers, artists and thinkers to skate into the corners with elbows up against aging, tired voices of American world domination. And gaining control of our economy does not mean simply trading U.S. capitalists for Canadian capitalists because by doing only that we would still be playing a game that we cannot win. Most capitalists, by definition, care primarily about money. They sell out to the highest bidder, which is often foreign, as owners of large steel, forestry, mining, oil and other companies have proven in recent years. In fact, the only industries that Canadian-owned companies still dominate are those in which the government restricts foreign ownership, such as telecommunications, media, railways and banking. And even in those industries capitalists lobby the government to allow them to sell out to the highest bidder.

The problem is not that our capitalists are sellouts or mostly pro-USA, even though they are. The problem is an economic system that is based on one-dollar one-vote, rather than one-person one-vote and a few rich Americans got a whole lot more dollars than all of us put together. The problem is ten percent of our population owns more than half of Canada's wealth (according to 2005 statistics) and that ten percent mostly sides with the American empire because it looks after its wealthy friends. The problem is an economic system in which a minority rules over the majority. In order to gain and maintain their power, ruling minorities have always divided and conquered the majority by playing up differences of ethnicity, religion and even geography. And that is incompatible with our dream of post-ethnic, democratic, internationalist nationalism.

The only way we can gain control of Canada is by building an economic system that is democratic. This doesn't necessarily mean government-owned in the way most people understand it. Rather, we need to create enterprises that are owned by the people who work in them and by the communities that depend on them for jobs. To do this we must expand our political democracy so that it is truly representative and then use that power to build cooperatives and community-owned, pension-fund-owned, city-owned, provincially-owned and federally-owned companies that operate under the control and direction of the people who work for them, together with representatives of the community, pension fund, city, provincial or federal government. Call such a system economic democracy. In addition to being good for us, it would allow us to create an economy that was independent of the U.S. and take away the power of their capitalists to run our country in their self-interest.

In good Canadian fashion our economic democracy would be a compromise between what most people call capitalism and socialism. We'd use the best of both systems. We'd build on our long history of government-owned enterprises, but we'd make them more democratic and continue to use the market to set most prices and to keep companies efficient. In addition to the cooperatives and community-worker-run larger enterprises, we would encourage a vibrant, innovative small and medium-size local business community. New immigrants are an especially good source for people who have the creativity to build these kinds of businesses. Immigrants are often "can-do" kinds of entrepreneurs who are not infected by the branch plant, colonial ideas of much of the old Canadian ruling class, whose greatest goal in life seems to be "selling out" for the largest sum of money available. Community-owned banks and credit unions would provide start-up capital to anyone with a good idea and a solid business plan. While there is a need for regulation, it should be designed to interfere as little as possible with creativity and individual initiative.

Economic democracy does not mean bigger, more bureaucratic government that discourages individual enterprise. The innovation and creativity of small business benefits us all, but when an enterprise becomes large the tendency under capitalism is to sell it off to the highest bidder, which is inevitably a giant corporation that is usually just as bureaucratic as any government. And more often than not it is foreign owned. If we lived in an economic democracy, when a company grew large enough the rules of worker and community control would take effect, rather than capitalism's rule of selling out to the highest bidder.

Just as the solutions to the problems of our Medicare system will be found in making it more democratic, rather than more like the American corporate-controlled system, the same will be true of the rest of our economy. We do need to fight bureaucracy, but the way to do it is by spreading out control to multiple owning communities and by empowering workers to make decisions. The best way to get rid of bureaucracy, corporate or governmental, is to give real power to the people who do the work. Workers must become owners either directly in medium-sized enterprises or through elected representatives who sit on company boards in larger companies. Decision-making should be a joint responsibility of the workers and communities or the cooperatives or pension funds or government that own the business. When workers are owners they will feel truly responsible, truly committed to success. When workers are owners who have real decision-making powers workplaces can be successfully run by the people who work in them, rather than managers reporting to a bureaucracy who in turn report to a corporate elite who report to a board which does the bidding of a few wealthy people, who are more often than not U.S. capitalists.

Building such an economic system will require a strong political will, which will only come from a shared vision uniting most of us around a common goal. We must dream big and then follow up that dream with action. That's what the ordinary people of Saskatchewan did when they elected a CCF government committed to creating the first every-one-included, single-payer, funded-by-taxes medical care system in North America. Canadian Medicare didn't just happen, it was built by the combined strength of hundreds of thousands of people working as one big team built by many smaller teams who came together through unions, farmers' cooperatives, political parties and many other organizations, despite the opposition of the rich and powerful.

Working together is the key. Moderately talented individuals playing as a team can beat those with greater talents but poorer teamwork, as everyone who follows hockey understands. Teamwork can make us greater than the sum of the individuals on our side. This is proved when a coach throws out his best three players and then is surprised to learn they don't make a very good line because there is no chemistry. The best line is one that works beyond the skill of three individual players, but rather creatively as a unit. The best lines include the players on them and the spaces between them. Having three or four great lines allows teams that draw on a much smaller pool of players to beat teams that can choose from ten times the population.

Canada must build an economic system that is based on teamwork. The necessary first step is that people who work together must feel part of a team. But how can you truly feel part of a team when your employer "owns" your job, when you are devalued and treated as a mere cog in a giant machine, when the boss makes all the important decisions, when the primary goal of your company is to send the most money possible to people you don't even know and are already rich? And, to make the alienation even more dramatic, when the rich owners of your company reside in another country?

We can do better than capitalism. Economic democracy is not some naïve dream. Cooperatives and credit unions have a long history in Canada. Federal, provincial and municipal governments do own critical parts of our economy. Producer co-ops were once quite common, until the apostles of greed convinced farmers and others to sell out for short-term gains (and long-term regret). Some corporations and other enterprises have experimented with forms of worker ownership and control. The idea of promoting local economies is growing throughout the world, especially in the realm of food production. There is even a "slow city" movement that encourages towns to promote local business and reject mass retailing.

If we once again go back to the roots of Canada when it was seen as the alternative to the USA, as better than the USA, then creating an economic democracy in this country makes even more sense. One way to think of the USA is as the "best of 1776," frozen in time. The goals of the American Revolution were independence and to create a modern political and economic system. They did so by the standards of 1776. At that time a feudal aristocracy was still the dominant class. An important debate of the framers of the new U.S. constitution was over how far democracy should go and whether or not an American aristocracy would be a good idea. While a formal aristocracy was not re-created, an "aristocracy of capitalists" was the true culmination of the American Revolution. The U.S. political system today is dominated by money and that inevitably means by a relatively few rich people. They have power at least comparable to the 18th century British aristocracy.

The distortions and limitations of the U.S. model of extreme capitalism are readily apparent. The economy is run like a feudal empire with property (mostly inherited) determining power. The so-called democracy of the U.S. government is always trumped by the power of a financial oligarchy that in reality runs the country. The modern Canadian alternative should be to strengthen political democracy and expand the principles of representative government into the economy. Everywhere people work together the default governing principle should be one-person, one-vote, rather than the one-dollar, one-vote current reality. That should be the economic game we play, rather than follow the rules of U.S. dominated capitalism.

Economic democracy is the logical outcome of the golden rule: We should treat others as we wish to be treated by them. We must be responsible and demand responsibility. We must all be co-owners. Even the apostles of greed agree that ownership equals responsibility. But they want to keep both in capitalists' hands.

What is the alternative to building an economic democracy that puts real power in the hands and brains of all citizens? Playing their game, which means more of the same — drifting along, becoming ever more part of the failing American capitalist system — until one day we wake up and realize we are them. Then having to wait decades more until everyone figures out that there has to be a better way. Why not start building the new, better world now? Why not take advantage of Canada's unique heritage that allows us to move forward as a beacon to the whole world? Why not be leaders rather than followers?

Or would we be better off as part of the United States? Some people think we could buy more slightly less overpriced beer at NHL or junior games, because their economy is bigger and more efficient, but I doubt most of us would have a higher standard of living. Sure some stuff is cheaper down there and the selection can be better, but their unions are weaker, their social services are worse, their medical care extremely expensive — all these things are part of the standard of living — so what I see is maybe 15% of Canadians at the top might be better off, but the other 85% of regular working folk would be poorer. Hell, Medicare, just by itself, is a good enough reason to keep Canada and not join the USA.

The truth is the USA is looking more and more like a "failed brand," as they say in the business world. Too many bad things are associated with its "franchise," including militarism, imperialism, corruption, extreme capitalism, an unhealthy food system, the dominance of automobiles, religious and economic fundamentalism, a disregard for others, ignorance, narrow mindedness and bullying — to name just a few.

But "enough already with the negativity," as a great Canadian actor playing a crazy (like a fox) tank commander said in a 1970s war movie called Kelly's Heroes. If the best reasons we can come up with for keeping Canada an independent country are variations on the theme of "my team is better than your team" then we really are conceding that there is no positive reason for Canada to exist and that we are just waiting for the time when our two countries' politics once again align in order to abandon our raison d'etre. Why not join up now and fight for what we believe from inside the belly of the American beast?

Another way of putting this: Are there some things at the core of Canada that are unique to us? Some things that are important, not just to us, but to all of humanity? Some things that elevate Canada from a nice place to live, all the way up to an important place on the planet where unique events have transpired, which allow us to inspire the world? Some things that could inspire us to truly become leaders? Like for example, to lead the world past old ethnic and national divisions, to an understanding that everyone must cooperate to heal our planet's environmental wounds, to teach the warmongers that there is a better way, to create an economic democracy?

The truth is we have one of the oldest continuous democracies in the world that has (more or less) peacefully united people speaking languages from the two countries that have fought more wars and conquered more colonies than any other nations on the planet over the past two and half centuries. That's an accomplishment best described as unique and inspiring. We are one of the very few places in the world where the displacement of aboriginal peoples was done (more or less) by "lawful" means that usually at least acknowledged the sovereignty of the first inhabitants, rather than by simple military conquest. We are a place where for almost two centuries the European "conquerors" in fact shared power with First Nations and to get ahead often meant marrying into the "right" native family. While Canada does have a shameful legacy of racism, colonialism, ethnic cleansing and cultural genocide we also do have a better record than most countries around the world that were "settled" by Europeans. Of course taking other people's land, while destroying their culture, could never be described as inspiring — except by primitive, ethno-centric cultures — but compared to standards of the time, Canada was a model of enlightenment. In addition, we have finally begun to acknowledge and deal with First Nations sovereignty. Our uniquely Canadian solutions are inspiring to many people around the world.

We established in earlier chapters that Canadians don't have a good definition of who we are, although we do acknowledge certain common characteristics. We constantly apologize and then say we're sorry that we're so polite. We're wishy-washy and make comprises to avoid conflict, but we're not really sorry about that. Instead, we're proud that we're pragmatic and try to get along.

When you think about it, this is a not bad starting point for building a post-ethnic, democratic, internationalist nationalism and an economic democracy. It is certainly a much better place than being certain you're the best in the world, wanting to dominate, seeing yourself as better than others and having declared a manifest destiny that tells the world you will dominate and control it. Those attitudes may be suitable for building an empire, but not for leading the world past racism, imperialism and war. Wanting to get along is a necessary first step in building an ethos of post-ethnic democratic internationalism and economic democracy. Politeness and always being willing to say you're sorry are not bad steps two and three. And not being certain of who you are enhances the possibility of becoming someone new.

We take pride in our sense of humour and think people who take themselves too seriously are probably only fit for a seat in the Senate where they can do others little harm. A willingness to laugh at yourself is always necessary when you undertake a project so serious as building a new and better world.

We've also established that Canadians have centuries of experience in dealing with minority rights, especially language. Our country was built through a process of destroying scores of First Nations, a fact that many of us have understood and have been working to overcome. While Canada is certainly not yet where it needs to be, at least we have decades of legal, political, cultural and emotional experience of dealing with our colonialism and racism. That could prove invaluable in many parts of the world where billions of people still suffer from the lingering effects of imperialism and its ideological justifications. And our legacy of language battles gives Canadians a unique perspective on the compromises necessary to create institutions that function in a multilingual world.

So, our historical "weaknesses," our lack of a clear definition of who we are, our tendency towards indecision and compromise and our willingness to poke fun at ourselves, are not problems to be overcome but rather the exact background needed for success in the project of building a better world. Loud, brash, twanged voices of manifest destiny may make fun of the very idea of post-ethnic internationalist nationalism or economic democracy and scoff at claims that Canada could lead the way, but that skepticism suits our project too. It is exactly the motivation needed to bind us together from coast to coast to coast. Nothing unites Canadians so well as right-wing Americans making fun of us.

We're sorry if that sounds anti-American, but it isn't really. We're just choosing to be different, to be ourselves. The world does not need another United States or an even more powerful United States that would result from it acquiring the rest of the North American continent. The world does not need another country that believes itself to be above all others or which promotes the notion that there is only one right way. The world does however need to be shown that it is possible for all people to live together, treating everyone with respect and dignity. Since that requires compromise, we should acknowledge its utility and promote its virtue. Since that also requires a sense of humour, we should first laugh at ourselves, then poke fun at the barriers that sometimes make us enemies, then build a comedy club that is the entire planet. Our Earth desperately needs all the people on it to love and care for their families, their towns, their regions and their countries, but also to love and care for the entire planet.

The world is crying out for post-ethnic, internationalist nationalists with a good sense of humour, with a willingness to compromise and whose only cherished absolute certainty is that no one is always right. Canada seems like a good choice to set up a training camp for players with exactly those qualities to play a game called "Let's Save the Planet" or at least "We Could Try Making the World A Better Place."

Truth is there's something that pisses me off even more than the price of NHL tickets. People who claim we are all just individuals and there's no such thing as the common good. Anyone who believes that should be banished to a place where there's no one else in a month's walking distance. Human beings are social creatures who rely on other people to survive and thrive. Anyone who says different is either a fool or a liar paid by powerful people to prevent ordinary people from taking collective action, which is the only kind that has any chance of success in making the world a better place.

# CHAPTER 9

# Looking forward

Our actions, our ideas, our choices, our interactions — immigrants and current Canadians — all will add up to produce an answer to the question "what is a Canadian" a hundred years from now when my granddaughter's granddaughters are writing advice for their granddaughters. And hopefully the answer will be that a good Canadian is someone who always tries his or her best to make the world a better place for all.

Building our new Canada will not be easy. In fact it will be complicated, but isn't this just another way of saying millions of people will play a part in how things turn out? Every immigrant who becomes a Canadian has taken a step on a long road. Every Canadian who comes to understand the debt we owe this land's original inhabitants for being so generous has played a part. Every current Canadian who assists a refugee to fit in, has shaped a piece of our future. Every immigrant who makes an effort to understand his or her new community has made a contribution. Every union or community leader who helps educate her or his membership to understand that we are all immigrants, and always have been, has played a key role. Every Canadian politician who votes to expand immigrant services has taken a step. Every current Canadian and immigrant who creates a partnership between some part of the world and Canada has changed our country forever. Every current Canadian and immigrant who helps create a sense of internationalism and common humanity has moved us closer to our goal. Everyone who strives to overcome stereotypes about "race" or ethnicity or religion has accomplished something significant. Everyone who insists on a policy of one-person one-vote in all areas of society, including the economy, has helped change our world. Everyone who promotes the idea of economic democracy has moved us further along the road to our preferred destination.

When the millions of new immigrants who will come to this country in the next decades have become citizens and their grandchildren and your grandchildren and my grandchildren have grown up together, what will these new Canadians be like? Will they look like us? Think like us? Act like us? Or will they be better than us? Will they have achieved a society that is post-ethnic, democratic and internationalist? What will Canada's place in the world be? Will people all around the planet see us as a beacon of what is possible? Will our descendents look back, thank us and say all the difficulties and turmoil we faced to create a better world was worth with it? But, most important of all, will immigration finally solve the Toronto problem or will the following generations look back and wonder, like we have, how the Maple Leafs can possibly go so long without winning a Stanley Cup?

History teaches us that there are no guarantees when

trying to figure out what the future might bring. But it also suggests that human agency can have a powerful impact on how things turn out. While we may not be able to choose our exact future, we can at least narrow the range of possible outcomes. If millions of people who become Canadian over the next few decades share some common aims with millions of current Canadians there is a strong possibility that those goals will have a powerful impact on the political and cultural life of the country. If enough of us want to create a post-ethnic, democratic, internationalist "Canadian nationalism" and an economic democracy we can probably do it.

But this kind of Canada won't be built from the top down. It will only happen as a process that grows from deep in the soil of every part of this great country. Ordinary, everyday, working Canadians must be convinced of the dream, then pass it on through their unions, their churches, their political parties, their local governments and their neighbourhood coffee shops until the vast majority of us believe in post-ethnic, democratic internationalism and economic democracy.

Looking to the future when our granddaughters' granddaughters are our ages, we can see the distant outline of a new nation that has moved beyond ethnicity and instead embraced a common humanity, which is thoroughly democratic and internationalist, which is widely acknowledged as the best place on the planet. While this place, stretched across the North American continent, is older, wiser and better than the Canada of today, it does resemble us.

# Ethnicity of Canada's cities

As a good coach of beginners, novice and atom teams would say: It's not whether you win or lose, but rather how you play the game — on the other hand, you can often tell the next Wayne Gretzky from the score sheet.

What follows is a list (from the 2006 census) of the top-20 ethnic groups in Canada and in every city with a population over 100,000. Each is given a "homogeneity score," which is calculated by determining the percentage that the largest ethnic group reported is of the total population and rounding that to a whole number. The lower the score, the more diverse is the population.

**Canada (Population 31,612,897)**
**Visible minorities: 16.2%**
**Homogeneity Score: 32**
**Ethnic Top 20**
**(includes multiple responses)**

| | |
|---|---|
| Canadian ........................ 10,066,290 | N. American Indian........ 1,253,615 |
| English .......................... 6,570,015 | Ukrainian........................ 1,209,085 |
| French ........................... 4,941,210 | Dutch (Netherlands) ...... 1,035,965 |
| Scottish.......................... 4,719,850 | Polish .............................. 984,565 |
| Irish ............................... 4,354,155 | East Indian ..................... 962,665 |
| German .......................... 3,179,425 | Russian ........................... 500,600 |
| Italian ............................ 1,445,335 | Welsh.............................. 440,965 |
| Chinese........................... 1,346,510 | Filipino ........................... 436,190 |
| | Norwegian ...................... 432,515 |
| | Portuguese ...................... 410,850 |
| | Metis .............................. 409,065 |
| | Other British Isles .......... 403,915 |

**1. Toronto (5,113,149)**
**Visible minorities: 42.9%**
**Homogeneity Score: 16**
**Ethnic Top 20**

| | |
|---|---|
| English | 804,100 |
| Canadian | 651,635 |
| Scottish | 561,050 |
| Chinese | 537,060 |
| Irish | 531,865 |
| East Indian | 484,655 |
| Italian | 466,155 |
| German | 259,015 |
| French | 241,395 |
| Polish | 207,495 |
| Portuguese | 188,110 |
| Filipino | 181,330 |
| Jamaican | 160,205 |
| Jewish | 141,685 |
| Ukrainian | 122,510 |
| Russian | 102,815 |
| Spanish | 97,255 |
| Dutch (Netherlands) | 95,560 |
| Greek | 90,585 |
| Sri Lankan | 80,610 |

**2. Montréal (3,635,571)**
**Visible minorities: 16.5%**
**Homogeneity Score: 46**
**Ethnic Top 20**

| | |
|---|---|
| Canadian | 1,670,655 |
| French | 936,990 |
| Italian | 260,345 |
| Irish | 216,410 |
| English | 148,095 |
| Scottish | 119,365 |
| Haitian | 85,785 |
| Chinese | 82,665 |
| German | 78,315 |
| N. American Indian | 74,565 |
| Québécois | 72,445 |
| Jewish | 68,485 |
| Greek | 61,770 |
| Spanish | 56,770 |
| Lebanese | 53,455 |
| Polish | 51,920 |
| Portuguese | 46,535 |
| East Indian | 39,305 |
| Romanian | 36,275 |
| Russian | 35,800 |

**3. Vancouver (2,116,581)**
**Visible minorities: 41.7%**
**Homogeneity Score: 23**
**Ethnic Top 20**

| | |
|---|---|
| English | 484,340 |
| Chinese | 402,000 |
| Scottish | 337,225 |
| Canadian | 278,350 |
| Irish | 251,695 |
| German | 203,720 |
| East Indian | 181,895 |
| French | 137,270 |
| Filipino | 83,765 |
| Ukrainian | 81,725 |
| Italian | 76,345 |
| Dutch (Netherlands) | 71,715 |
| Polish | 60,715 |
| Russian | 47,940 |
| Norwegian | 46,260 |
| Korean | 46,035 |
| N. American Indian | 43,190 |
| Welsh | 41,805 |
| Swedish | 39,920 |
| Spanish | 36,000 |

## 4. Ottawa-Gatineau (1,130,761)
**Visible minorities: 16.0%**
**Homogeneity Score: 37**
**Ethnic Top 20**

| | |
|---|---|
| Canadian | 419,805 |
| French | 291,735 |
| English | 219,490 |
| Irish | 213,475 |
| Scottish | 176,725 |
| German | 79,835 |
| Italian | 45,005 |
| N. American Indian | 39,440 |
| Chinese | 36,605 |
| Polish | 28,585 |
| Dutch (Netherlands) | 25,575 |
| Lebanese | 24,530 |
| Other British Isles | 22,550 |
| Ukrainian | 21,520 |
| East Indian | 21,170 |
| Welsh | 16,125 |
| Jewish | 12,495 |
| Metis | 12,215 |
| Portuguese | 12,045 |
| Russian | 11,945 |

## 5. Calgary (1,079,310)
**Visible minorities: 22.2%**
**Homogeneity Score: 27**
**Ethnic Top 20**

| | |
|---|---|
| English | 291,370 |
| Scottish | 223,000 |
| Canadian | 207,790 |
| German | 182,940 |
| Irish | 175,575 |
| French | 109,180 |
| Ukrainian | 76,240 |
| Chinese | 75,410 |
| East Indian | 48,270 |
| Polish | 47,925 |
| Dutch (Netherlands) | 47,650 |
| Norwegian | 35,935 |
| Italian | 33,645 |
| Russian | 30,975 |
| Filipino | 26,680 |
| N. American Indian | 26,110 |
| Welsh | 25,935 |
| Swedish | 25,410 |
| Other British Isles | 23,205 |
| American | 22,015 |

## 6. Edmonton (1,034,945)
**Visible minorities: 17.1%**
**Homogeneity Score: 24**
**Ethnic Top 20**

| | |
|---|---|
| English | 252,955 |
| German | 196,575 |
| Scottish | 194,185 |
| Canadian | 192,410 |
| Irish | 165,590 |
| Ukrainian | 144,620 |
| French | 131,225 |
| Polish | 67,520 |
| Chinese | 53,670 |
| Dutch (Netherlands) | 49,280 |
| N. American Indian | 45,600 |
| Norwegian | 39,045 |
| East Indian | 34,605 |
| Italian | 28,805 |
| Swedish | 28,225 |
| Metis | 27,130 |
| Russian | 24,425 |
| Welsh | 23,165 |
| Filipino | 21,150 |
| American | 17,380 |

## 7. Québec City (715,515)
**Visible minorities: 2.3%**
**Homogeneity Score: 70**
**Ethnic Top 20**

| | |
|---|---|
| Canadian | 502,845 |
| French | 245,840 |
| Irish | 33,450 |
| N. American Indian | 13,765 |
| Scottish | 13,605 |
| Québécois | 13,000 |
| English | 10,295 |
| German | 8,555 |
| Italian | 7,410 |
| Spanish | 3,675 |
| Acadian | 3,280 |
| Belgian | 3,185 |
| American | 2,735 |
| Portuguese | 2,395 |
| Chinese | 2,245 |
| Metis | 1,850 |
| Polish | 1,475 |
| Swiss | 1,410 |
| Colombian | 1,335 |
| African | 1,330 |

## 8. Winnipeg (694,668)
**Visible minorities: 15.0%**
**Homogeneity Score: 22**
**Ethnic Top 20**

| | |
|---|---|
| English | 156,290 |
| Scottish | 126,740 |
| German | 121,565 |
| Canadian | 117,225 |
| Ukrainian | 110,335 |
| French | 97,410 |
| Irish | 95,185 |
| Polish | 58,050 |
| Metis | 42,175 |
| Filipino | 38,275 |
| N. American Indian | 36,515 |
| Dutch (Netherlands) | 30,310 |
| Russian | 23,385 |
| Italian | 18,580 |
| Icelandic | 17,655 |
| Chinese | 16,695 |
| East Indian | 13,545 |
| Swedish | 13,470 |
| Jewish | 12,210 |
| Welsh | 11,350 |

## 9. Hamilton (692,911)
**Visible minorities: 12.3%**
**Homogeneity Score: 30**
**Ethnic Top 20**

| | |
|---|---|
| English | 205,570 |
| Canadian | 152,655 |
| Scottish | 143,320 |
| Irish | 119,085 |
| Italian | 72,440 |
| German | 67,395 |
| French | 60,075 |
| Polish | 37,365 |
| Dutch (Netherlands) | 37,355 |
| Ukrainian | 27,080 |
| Portuguese | 17,095 |
| Hungarian (Magyar) | 15,155 |
| East Indian | 14,985 |
| Other British Isles | 14,835 |
| N. American Indian | 14,370 |
| Welsh | 13,875 |
| Chinese | 13,600 |
| Croatian | 12,120 |
| Serbian | 7,960 |
| Russian | 7,315 |

**10. London (457,720)**
**Visible minorities: 11.1%**
**Homogeneity Score: 35**
**Ethnic Top 20**
English ............................ 157,960
Canadian ........................ 120,055
Scottish........................... 107,705
Irish ................................. 91,675
German ........................... 54,350
French ............................. 45,150
Dutch (Netherlands) ...... 32,840
Italian ............................. 20,380
Polish.............................. 19,395
Portuguese ...................... 12,465
Ukrainian........................ 10,765
N. American Indian........ 10,355
Other British Isle ........... 10,145
Welsh.............................. 9,315
Chinese........................... 7,960
Hungarian (Magyar) ...... 7,300
East Indian ...................... 5,395
American......................... 5,250
Belgian............................ 4,700
Russian ........................... 4,690

**11. Kitchener-Waterloo (451,235)**
**Visible minorities: 13.8%**
**Homogeneity Score: 26**
**Ethnic Top 20**
English ............................ 115,885
Canadian ........................ 110,945
German ........................... 105,670
Scottish........................... 83,845
Irish ................................. 77,500
French ............................. 42,070
Polish.............................. 22,105
Dutch (Netherlands) ...... 21,020

Portuguese ...................... 19,500
Italian ............................. 13,675
East Indian ...................... 13,235
Chinese........................... 10,970
Ukrainian........................ 10,425
Other British Isles .......... 9,255
North American Indian.. 8,775
Romanian ........................ 7,910
Hungarian (Magyar) ...... 7,885
Welsh.............................. 7,080
Swiss................................ 5,630
Russian ........................... 5,250

**12. St. Catharines (385,035)**
**Visible minorities: 6.6%**
**Homogeneity Score: 31**
**Ethnic Top 20**
English ............................ 119,235
Canadian ........................ 96,910
Scottish........................... 75,860
Irish ................................. 66,895
German ........................... 57,300
French ............................. 51,065
Italian ............................. 48,850
Dutch (Netherlands) ...... 27,700
Ukrainian........................ 20,990
Polish.............................. 18,505
Hungarian (Magyar) ...... 11,635
N. American Indian........ 11,260
Welsh.............................. 7,650
Other British Isles .......... 7,055
American......................... 5,420
Russian ........................... 5,120
Chinese........................... 4,635
Spanish ........................... 3,575
East Indian ...................... 3,165
Croatian.......................... 2,805

**13. Halifax (372,858)**
**Visible minorities: 7.5%**
**Homogeneity Score: 37**
**Ethnic Top 20**

| | |
|---|---|
| Canadian | 139,060 |
| English | 126,250 |
| Scottish | 110,085 |
| Irish | 90,675 |
| French | 66,415 |
| German | 44,630 |
| Dutch (Netherlands) | 14,645 |
| N. American Indian | 12,740 |
| Welsh | 8,220 |
| Other British Isles | 7,045 |
| Italian | 6,700 |
| Polish | 5,380 |
| Acadian | 5,270 |
| Ukrainian | 4,030 |
| Lebanese | 3,895 |
| Chinese | 3,720 |
| African | 3,475 |
| Black | 3,205 |
| American | 2,940 |
| East Indian | 2,780 |

**14. Oshawa (330,594)**
**Visible minorities: 10.3%**
**Homogeneity Score: 35**
**Ethnic Top 20**

| | |
|---|---|
| English | 116,015 |
| Canadian | 102,380 |
| Scottish | 77,975 |
| Irish | 75,550 |
| French | 36,610 |
| German | 28,595 |
| Italian | 18,225 |
| Dutch (Netherlands) | 17,290 |
| Polish | 13,420 |
| Ukrainian | 12,555 |
| North American Indian | 8,980 |
| Other British Isles | 7,590 |
| Welsh | 7,330 |
| Jamaican | 7,065 |
| Portuguese | 6,530 |
| East Indian | 5,675 |
| Chinese | 5,170 |
| Hungarian (Magyar) | 4,240 |
| Spanish | 3,525 |
| Greek | 3,430 |

**15. Victoria (330,088)**
**Visible minorities: 10.4%**
**Homogeneity Score: 43**
**Ethnic Top 20**

| | |
|---|---|
| English | 142,165 |
| Scottish | 92,480 |
| Canadian | 69,990 |
| Irish | 66,655 |
| German | 43,625 |
| French | 33,230 |
| Dutch (Netherlands) | 15,595 |
| Ukrainian | 15,020 |
| Chinese | 13,550 |
| Welsh | 13,195 |
| N. American Indian | 12,045 |
| Norwegian | 11,180 |
| Polish | 10,895 |
| Italian | 9,450 |
| Swedish | 8,805 |
| Other British Isles | 8,780 |
| American | 6,895 |
| Russian | 6,720 |
| East Indian | 6,550 |
| Danish | 5,520 |

### 16. Windsor (323,342)
**Visible minorities: 16.0%**
**Homogeneity Score: 26**
**Ethnic Top 20**

Canadian ........................ 85,170
French ............................ 81,230
English ........................... 70,920
Irish ................................ 49,670
Scottish........................... 45,170
Italian ............................ 33,725
German .......................... 31,605
Polish.............................. 13,420
Ukrainian........................ 9,725
N. American Indian........ 9,680
Lebanese.......................... 9,035
Chinese........................... 8,830
Dutch (Netherlands) ...... 8,585
East Indian ..................... 7,260
Hungarian (Magyar) ...... 6,950
Romanian ....................... 5,650
American......................... 4,440
Croatian.......................... 4,095
Serbian ........................... 3,915
Welsh.............................. 3,600

### 17. Saskatoon (233,923)
**Visible minorities: 6.4%**
**Homogeneity Score: 31**
**Ethnic Top 20**

German .......................... 72,185
English ........................... 62,285
Scottish........................... 46,640
Canadian ........................ 39,895
Ukrainian........................ 38,825
Irish ................................ 37,400
French ............................ 29,715
Norwegian...................... 17,195

N. American Indian........ 15,875
Polish.............................. 14,505
Dutch (Netherlands) ...... 11,260
Russian ........................... 10,960
Metis .............................. 9,125
Swedish .......................... 7,710
Hungarian (Magyar) ...... 5,760
Welsh.............................. 5,155
Chinese........................... 4,965
American......................... 3,205
Austrian.......................... 3,120
Other British Isles .......... 2,945

### 18. Regina (194,971)
**Visible minorities: 6.6%**
**Homogeneity Score: 33**
**Ethnic Top 20**

German .......................... 64,240
English ........................... 52,710
Scottish........................... 40,635
Canadian ........................ 33,715
Irish ................................ 33,145
Ukrainian........................ 25,725
French ............................ 22,095
N. American Indian........ 12,660
Polish.............................. 12,555
Norwegian...................... 10,810
Hungarian (Magyar) ...... 8,420
Metis .............................. 6,610
Russian ........................... 6,575
Austrian.......................... 6,455
Swedish .......................... 5,800
Dutch (Netherlands) ...... 5,705
Romanian ....................... 5,040
Welsh.............................. 4,120
Chinese........................... 3,865
Italian ............................ 2,565

## 19. Sherbrooke (186,952)
**Visible minorities: 3.8%**
**Homogeneity Score: 68**
**Ethnic Top 20**

| | |
|---|---|
| Canadian | 128,040 |
| French | 59,285 |
| Irish | 11,190 |
| English | 6,555 |
| N. American Indian | 5,785 |
| Scottish | 3,785 |
| Québécois | 3,090 |
| German | 2,890 |
| Italian | 2,360 |
| Belgian | 1,400 |
| Spanish | 1,185 |
| American | 1,185 |
| Chinese | 785 |
| Metis | 785 |
| Acadian | 705 |
| Polish | 645 |
| Afghan | 585 |
| Colombian | 560 |
| Salvadorean | 490 |
| Moroccan | 465 |

## 20. St. John's (181,113)
**Visible minorities: 1.9%**
**Homogeneity Score: 45**
**Ethnic Top 20**

| | |
|---|---|
| English | 80,690 |
| Canadian | 77,980 |
| Irish | 56,875 |
| Scottish | 15,595 |
| French | 8,865 |
| German | 4,010 |
| N. American Indian | 3,505 |
| Newfoundlander | 2,455 |
| Other British Isles | 1,905 |
| Welsh | 1,845 |
| Inuit | 1,245 |
| Chinese | 1,165 |
| Dutch (Netherlands) | 1,085 |
| Norwegian | 875 |
| Metis | 855 |
| Italian | 795 |
| East Indian | 670 |
| American | 630 |
| Portuguese | 615 |
| Swedish | 545 |

## 21. Barrie (177,061)
**Visible minorities: 5.8%**
**Homogeneity Score: 37**
**Ethnic Top 20**

| | |
|---|---|
| English | 65,155 |
| Canadian | 58,510 |
| Scottish | 45,305 |
| Irish | 41,385 |
| French | 23,050 |
| German | 18,920 |
| Italian | 10,330 |
| Dutch (Netherlands) | 9,575 |
| Polish | 6,950 |
| Ukrainian | 5,920 |
| N. American Indian | 5,410 |
| Other British Isles | 4,730 |
| Welsh | 4,160 |
| Portuguese | 2,610 |
| Hungarian (Magyar) | 2,100 |
| American | 1,890 |
| East Indian | 1,830 |
| Metis | 1,830 |
| Spanish | 1,805 |
| Finnish | 1,685 |

**22. Kelowna (162,276)**
**Visible minorities: 5.2%**
**Homogeneity Score: 34**
**Ethnic Top 20**
English ........................... 54,570
German .......................... 38,540
Scottish........................... 37,870
Canadian ........................ 33,765
Irish ................................ 28,205
French ............................ 18,960
Ukrainian........................ 13,425
Dutch (Netherlands) ...... 9,305
Polish.............................. 8,235
Norwegian ...................... 6,815
Russian ........................... 6,720
Italian ............................. 6,635
N. American Indian........ 5,940
Swedish .......................... 4,985
Welsh.............................. 4,675
Metis .............................. 3,200
Other British Isles .......... 2,995
Hungarian (Magyar) ...... 2,930
American......................... 2,740
Danish ............................ 2,685

**23. Abbotsford (159,020)**
**Visible minorities: 22.8%**
**Homogeneity Score: 27**
**Ethnic Top 20**
English ........................... 42,190
German .......................... 32,575
Canadian ........................ 30,415
Scottish........................... 28,700
East Indian ..................... 23,440
Irish ................................ 21,425
Dutch (Netherlands) ...... 16,645
French ............................ 13,725

Ukrainian........................ 8,090
Russian ........................... 7,420
N. American Indian........ 5,340
Polish.............................. 4,940
Norwegian ...................... 4,715
Swedish .......................... 4,245
Italian ............................. 3,675
Welsh.............................. 3,670
Metis .............................. 2,670
Chinese........................... 2,585
American......................... 2,320
Other British Isles .......... 2,270

**24. Sudbury (157,857)**
**Visible minorities: 2.1%**
**Homogeneity Score: 41**
**Ethnic Top 20**
Canadian ........................ 64,350
French ............................ 62,495
English ........................... 35,740
Irish ................................ 30,430
Scottish........................... 26,595
Italian ............................. 13,415
German .......................... 12,145
N. American Indian........ 8,525
Ukrainian........................ 7,585
Finnish ........................... 7,280
Metis .............................. 6,325
Polish.............................. 4,750
Dutch (Netherlands) ...... 2,890
Other British Isle ........... 1,775
Welsh.............................. 1,775
Swedish .......................... 1,625
American......................... 1,150
Croatian.......................... 1,015
Russian ........................... 930
Hungarian (Magyar) ...... 805

## 25. Kingston (152,358)
**Visible minorities: 5.8%**
**Homogeneity Score: 35**
**Ethnic Top 20**

| | |
|---|---|
| English | 52,600 |
| Canadian | 52,220 |
| Irish | 41,040 |
| Scottish | 39,060 |
| French | 22,790 |
| German | 14,445 |
| Dutch (Netherlands) | 9,305 |
| N. American Indian | 5,320 |
| Italian | 3,940 |
| Other British Isles | 3,880 |
| Polish | 3,675 |
| Welsh | 3,510 |
| Portuguese | 3,420 |
| Ukrainian | 2,655 |
| Chinese | 2,585 |
| American | 1,730 |
| East Indian | 1,520 |
| Metis | 1,280 |
| Danish | 1,175 |
| Greek | 1,155 |

## 26. Saguenay (151,643)
**Visible minorities: 0.9%**
**Homogeneity Score: 78**
**Ethnic Top 20**

| | |
|---|---|
| Canadian | 117,780 |
| French | 45,535 |
| Irish | 4,510 |
| N. American Indian | 4,225 |
| Québécois | 3,120 |
| Scottish | 2,740 |
| English | 1,845 |
| Metis | 1,620 |
| German | 865 |
| Acadian | 815 |
| Italian | 675 |
| Norwegian | 460 |
| Chinese | 330 |
| Belgian | 330 |
| American | 300 |
| Colombian | 225 |
| Portuguese | 220 |
| Polish | 215 |
| Spanish | 175 |
| Dutch (Netherlands) | 170 |

## 27. Guelph (127,010)
**Visible minorities: 12.7%**
**Homogeneity Score: 34**
**Ethnic Top 20**

| | |
|---|---|
| English | 42,720 |
| Canadian | 32,595 |
| Scottish | 32,295 |
| Irish | 27,630 |
| German | 18,495 |
| Italian | 12,110 |
| French | 11,585 |
| Dutch (Netherlands) | 7,720 |
| Polish | 4,915 |
| Chinese | 4,055 |
| Welsh | 3,250 |
| Other British Isles | 3,215 |
| East Indian | 2,935 |
| Hungarian (Magyar) | 2,920 |
| Ukrainian | 2,860 |
| N. American Indian | 2,320 |
| Filipino | 2,030 |
| Spanish | 1,465 |
| American | 1,450 |
| Vietnamese | 1,260 |

**28. Moncton (126,424)**
**Visible minorities: 2.0%**
**Homogeneity Score: 51**
**Ethnic Top 20**
Canadian .......................... 64,665
French ............................. 39,675
English ............................ 33,430
Scottish............................ 24,225
Irish ................................ 23,010
Acadian ............................ 8,075
German ............................ 8,040
N. American Indian........ 3,265
Dutch (Netherlands) ...... 2,010
Other British Isles .......... 1,585
Welsh................................ 1,325
Italian .............................. 1,295
Metis .................................. 745
American ............................ 740
Polish.................................. 605
Spanish ............................... 480
Chinese................................ 445
African................................ 425
Ukrainian............................ 420
Danish ................................ 415

**29. Trois-Rivières (126,323)**
**Visible minorities: 1.6%**
**Homogeneity Score: 83**
**Ethnic Top 20**
Canadian ........................ 104,795
French ............................. 43,980
Irish .................................. 5,205
N. American Indian........ 3,730
Québécois........................ 2,675
Scottish.............................. 1,915
English .............................. 1,900
German ............................. 1,445

Italian ................................ 980
Acadian .............................. 750
Spanish ............................... 620
American ............................ 590
Belgian................................ 580
Swiss................................... 385
Metis .................................. 345
Greek.................................. 330
Colombian.......................... 270
Chinese................................ 255
African................................ 220
Moroccan ........................... 215

**30. Brantford (124,607)**
**Visible minorities: 5.5%**
**Homogeneity Score: 37**
**Ethnic Top 20**
English ............................. 46,425
Canadian .......................... 36,445
Scottish............................. 29,285
Irish ................................. 23,415
German ............................. 15,275
French .............................. 11,410
Dutch (Netherlands) ....... 9,020
Polish................................. 6,845
Italian ............................... 6,695
N. American Indian........ 5,215
Ukrainian.......................... 4,760
Hungarian (Magyar) ...... 4,270
Welsh................................. 2,760
Other British Isles .......... 2,435
Portuguese ........................ 1,880
East Indian ....................... 1,540
American ............................ 1,450
Chinese................................ 1,120
Russian ............................... 935
Belgian................................ 890

## 31. Thunder Bay (122,907)
**Visible minorities: 2.7%**
**Homogeneity Score: 28**
**Ethnic Top 20**

| | |
|---|---|
| English | 34,355 |
| Scottish | 26,400 |
| Canadian | 24,650 |
| Irish | 22,260 |
| French | 21,130 |
| Ukrainian | 17,620 |
| Italian | 17,290 |
| Finnish | 14,510 |
| German | 13,085 |
| N. American Indian | 9,330 |
| Polish | 8,595 |
| Swedish | 5,585 |
| Dutch (Netherlands) | 4,825 |
| Norwegian | 3,890 |
| Slovak | 2,660 |
| Metis | 2,620 |
| Welsh | 2,510 |
| Other British Isles | 1,505 |
| Danish | 1,385 |
| Chinese | 1,180 |

## 32. Saint John (122,907)
**Visible minorities: 3.1%**
**Homogeneity Score: 41**
**Ethnic Top 20**

| | |
|---|---|
| Canadian | 50,915 |
| English | 43,030 |
| Irish | 40,620 |
| Scottish | 33,050 |
| French | 27,390 |
| German | 7,215 |
| Dutch (Netherlands) | 3,815 |
| N. American Indian | 3,810 |
| Welsh | 2,465 |
| Other British Isles | 1,565 |
| Italian | 1,315 |
| Chinese | 1,090 |
| Acadian | 1,025 |
| American | 1,010 |
| Danish | 945 |
| Lebanese | 905 |
| Swedish | 730 |
| Polish | 620 |
| Ukrainian | 565 |
| East Indian | 555 |

## 33. Peterborough (116,570)
**Visible minorities: 2.7%**
**Homogeneity Score: 41**
**Ethnic Top 20**

| | |
|---|---|
| English | 47,765 |
| Canadian | 39,350 |
| Irish | 35,925 |
| Scottish | 30,715 |
| French | 13,995 |
| German | 11,100 |
| Dutch (Netherlands) | 6,405 |
| N. American Indian | 4,720 |
| Italian | 4,470 |
| Polish | 2,700 |
| Other British Isles | 2,700 |
| Welsh | 2,700 |
| Ukrainian | 1,705 |
| Metis | 1,350 |
| American | 1,315 |
| Chinese | 890 |
| Danish | 765 |
| Russian | 760 |
| Hungarian (Magyar) | 735 |
| Austrian | 675 |

# About the author

Ernesto (Ernie) Raj Peshkov-Chow is a left-wing, union-loving, working-class, multi-generational Canadian who occasionally inhabits the brain of a long-time journalist at one of Canada's largest media outlets. Some say he is a socialist Don Cherry, but he prefers to describe himself as Saskatchewan's Charlie Farquharson.